BETHANY
COLLEGE
LIBRARY

**DISCARDED**

809.3876 OL8EL
Olsen, Lance, 1956-
Ellipse of uncertainty

GAYLORD S

# ELLIPSE
# OF
# UNCERTAINTY

Recent Titles in
Contributions to the Study of Science Fiction and Fantasy
Series Editor: Marshall Tymn

The Return from Avalon: A Study of the Arthurian Legend in Modern Fiction
*Raymond H. Thompson*

The Comedy of the Fantastic: Ecological Perspectives on the Fantasy Novel
*Don D. Elgin*

The Scope of the Fantastic—Culture, Biography, Themes, Children's Literature: Selected Essays from the First International Conference on the Fantastic in Literature and Film
*Robert A. Collins and Howard D. Pearce, editors*

Some Kind of Paradise: The Emergence of American Science Fiction
*Thomas D. Clareson*

The Unexpected Universe of Doris Lessing: A Study in Narrative Technique
*Katherine Fishburn*

Erotic Universe: Sexuality and Fantastic Literature
*Donald Palumbo, editor*

Aspects of Fantasy: Selected Essays from the Second International Conference on the Fantastic in Literature and Film
*William Coyle, editor*

Forms of the Fantastic: Selected Essays from the Third International Conference on the Fantastic in Literature and Film
*Jan Hokenson and Howard Pearce, editors*

Eros in the Mind's Eye: Sexuality and the Fantastic in Art and Film
*Donald Palumbo, editor*

Worlds Within Women: Myth and Mythmaking in Fantastic Literature by Women
*Thelma J. Shinn*

Reflections on the Fantastic: Selected Essays from the Fourth International Conference on the Fantastic in the Arts
*Michael R. Collings, Editor*

Merlin's Daughters: Contemporary Women Writers of Fantasy
*Charlotte Spivack*

# Ellipse of Uncertainty
## AN INTRODUCTION TO POSTMODERN FANTASY

Lance Olsen

CONTRIBUTIONS TO THE STUDY OF SCIENCE FICTION
AND FANTASY, NUMBER 26

**GREENWOOD PRESS**
NEW YORK · WESTPORT, CONNECTICUT · LONDON

Library of Congress Cataloging-in-Publication Data

Olsen, Lance, 1956–
   Ellipse of uncertainty.

   (Contributions to the study of science fiction and
fantasy, ISSN 0193-6875 ; no. 26)
   Bibliography: p.
   Includes index.
   1. Fantastic literature—History and criticism.
2. Postmodernism.   3. Literature, Modern—20th century—
History and criticism.   I. Title.   II. Series.
PN56.F34047   1987        809.3′876       86-22789
ISBN 0-313-25511-3 (lib. bdg. : alk. paper)

Copyright © 1987 by Lance Olsen

All right reseved. No portion of this book may be
reproduced, by any process or technique, without the
express written consent of the publisher.

Library of Congress Catalog Card Number: 86-22789
ISBN: 0-313-25511-3
ISSN: 0193-6875

First published in 1987

Greenwood Press, Inc.
88 Post Road West, Westport, Connecticut 06881

Printed in the United States of America

The paper used in this book complies with the
Permanent Paper Standard issued by the National
Information Standards Organization (Z39.48-1984).

10 9 8 7 6 5 4 3 2 1

**Copyright Acknowledgments**

An earlier version of chapter one appeared in *Extrapolation*; of chapter two in *Modern Language Studies*; of chapter four in *Review of Contemporary Fiction*; of chapter five in *Canadian Review of American Studies*; of chapter six in *Kansas Quarterly*; of chapter seven in *Ariel*. All are reprinted by permission.

The following publishers have generously given permission to use extended quotations from copyrighted works:

"Thanksgiving for a Habitat," from W.H. Auden: Collected Poems, edited by Edward Mendelson. Copyright © 1979 by Random House, Inc. Reprinted by permission.

From *Waiting for the Barbarians* by J.M. Coetzee. Copyright © 1980 by J.M. Coetzee. Reprinted by permission of Viking Penguin, Inc.

Excerpts from *Aura* by Carlos Fuentes. English translation copyright © 1965 by Carlos Fuentes. Reprinted by permission of Farrar, Straus, and Giroux, Inc., and Brandt & Brandt Literary Agents, Inc.

From *One Hundred Years of Solitude* by Gabriel García Márquez. Translated by Gregory Rabassa. Translation copyright © 1970 by Harper and Row Publishers, Inc. Reprinted by permission of Harper and Row Publishers, Inc., and Jonathan Cape, Ltd.

From *The Crying of Lot 49* by Thomas Pynchon. Copyright © 1966, 1965, by Thomas Pynchon. Reprinted by permission of Harper and Row Publishers, Inc., and Jonathan Cape, Ltd.

For Andrea, Always and All Ways

# Contents

| | |
|---|---|
| *Acknowledgments* | xi |
| 1. Prelude: Nameless Things and Thingless Names | 1 |
| 2. Diagnosing Fantastic Autism: Kafka, Borges, and Robbe-Grillet | 25 |
| 3. I Stink, Therefore I (S)am: Functions, Fantasy, and Beckett | 39 |
| 4. Metamorphosis and Fuentes' *Aura* | 51 |
| 5. Pynchon's New Nature: Indeterminacy and *The Crying of Lot 49* | 69 |
| 6. Misfires in Eden: García Márquez and Narrative Frustration | 85 |
| 7. The Presence of Absence: Coetzee's *Waiting for the Barbarians* | 101 |
| 8. Postlude | 115 |
| *Bibliography* | 119 |
| *Index* | 127 |

# *Acknowledgments*

Myriad thanks to Douglas Day for his seminar at the University of Virginia in the spring of 1983 that got all this started, and for his help in carrying it through. I greatly appreciate both Daniel Albright's and Walter Sokel's exquisite scrutiny of style and thought, and their excellent suggestions. Bless Guy Davenport for answering more silly questions than he realized; Roger C. Schlobin for taking me under wing; Allienne Becker for introducing me to the world of fantasts; Sheldon Laviano for lending me an ear when I needed it; Patricia Troxel and Arthur Wrobel for their ideas and their patience with me during the manuscript preparation; James Baker Hall, Patrick and Lalita Hogan, Marcia Hurlow, Gurney Norman, Ellen Rosenman, Greg Stump, and David Troxel for lending support in a multitude of ways throughout my work here. Bless Bob Hemenway, Kevin Kiernan, and the University of Kentucky for reducing my teaching load and granting me a summer research fellowship during the writing of this piece. And bless Andrea most of all, who helped make this book at least as much hers as mine.

# ELLIPSE
# OF
# UNCERTAINTY

# 1

# *Prelude: Nameless Things and Thingless Names*

> Yes, even then, when already all was fading, waves and particles, there could be no things but nameless things, no names but thingless names.
> — Beckett (*Molloy*, 31)

Suggesting that what Alain Robbe-Grillet somewhat misleadingly calls the Balzacian mode of fiction (a mode primarily interested in content; the communal; the psychological; the chronological; the fully rounded character; the mimetic—a mode, in other words, firmly grounded in "the world") is dead seems a little like suggesting there are no such things as UFOs. As much as one would like to believe or not in such charming and marvelous ideas, the fact remains that the *National Enquirer* and the U.S. Air Force report and catalog sightings continually. Competent writers working under realist, naturalist, and even modernist assumptions are presently alive, well, popular, and often financially successful, and their fiction, as Fredric Jameson points out, "persuades us in a concrete fashion that human actions, human life is somehow a complete, interlocking whole, a single, formed, meaningful substance. . . . Our satisfaction with the completeness of plot is therefore a kind of satisfaction with society as well" (12).

But alongside these modes, roughly since the 1940's, what has come for better or worse to be called postmodernism has surfaced. This mode of discourse agrees with Robbe-Grillet that such previous composition is reactionary, "no longer anything but an empty formula, serving only as the basis for tiresome parodies" (*For a New Novel*, 135). For him, "the novel of characters belongs entirely to the past, it describes a period: that which marked the apogee of the individual" (28); "the old myths of 'depth' " (23) are useless for describing mankind's current conception of self; the ideas of communal time and space and "reality" are fictions; and the universe "is neither significant nor absurd" (19).

In his well-known essay, "The Literature of Exhaustion," John Barth furthers this notion by suggesting that contemporary culture has entered into a state of "used-upness of certain forms or exhaustion of certain possibilities" (29). Just as "Beethoven's Sixth Symphony or the Chartres Cathedral if executed today would be merely embarrassing," he continues, so is the "turn-of-the-century-type" novel simply written "in more or less mid-twentieth-century language." In fact, "to be technically *out* of date is likely to be a serious defect" since "art and its forms and techniques live in history" (30) and so must change to reflect changes in historical consciousness. Rewriting the nineteenth- and early twentieth-century novel as our civilization swings into the last few years before the twenty-first reduces one to producing banal imitations, the argument goes. But " 'the literature of exhausted possibility'—or, more chicly, 'the literature of exhaustion' " is "by no means necessarily a cause for despair" (29) because it frees one up to search for new strategies or, more precisely, new combinations of old strategies.

One strategy that has been employed frequently by postmodern literature as a way to liberate its imagination from the realist, naturalist, and modernist modes of fiction is the fantastic. A mode that has been around since *The Epic of Gilgamesh*, which has been used for a variety of purposes (didactic, escapist, and so on), and which has often been considered a relatively minor genre, now fantasy has begun to compete with the Balzacian mode as the dominant form of fiction. Jean Kennard has gone so far as to argue that fantasy techniques "most of all characterize contemporary fiction. . . . [I]ndeed in the 1960s they became the rule rather than the exception" (10–11).

The result, as we shall see, is the creation of a particularly suitable vehicle for the postmodern imagination since contemporary fantasy may be thought of as the literary equivalent of deconstructionism. It is a mode which interrogates all we take for granted about language and experience, giving these no more than shifting and provisional status. It is a mode of radical skepticism that believes only in the impossibility of total intelligibility; in the endless displacement of "meaning"; in the production of a universe without "truth"; in a bottomless relativity of "significance."

Before examining these assertions more closely, I should like to emphasize that just as every narrative strategy suggests a metaphysical one so, too, does every critical strategy. Through this optic, every piece of criticism becomes as well a piece of spiritual autobiography. What I should like to underscore about my own is that it is *not* an apology for postmodern fantasy, but a description of it. In fact, many of the critical strategies I employ—the notions of genre, history, and psychology, for instance—are in direct opposition to the deconstructive impulse of postmodern fantasy. This essay shall not use deconstructive principles in its attempt to make the texts and the ideas it discusses more interesting and enjoyable (the end, it seems to me, of any piece of criticism), but it does create a dialogue with them in order to illuminate their presence.

At the same time, I should like to point out that at the heart of both deconstructivist orthodoxy and postmodern fantasy is a deep ambivalence with their own premises, an oscillation at least and a contradiction at most between their affirmation resulting in their philosophical commitment to the freeplay that leads to a deconstruction of self and world, and their nostalgia and commitment to the self that leads to a dread of pure freedom and a dream of some kind of limits (see Caramello's *Silverless Mirrors*). After all, a Derrida or Beckett who literally believed in the deconstructive turn, who literally believed in the dissolution of self, world, and language, would be philosophically obliged to stop writing and hence stop signing his name into the world of publication. Yet each continues to generate a self that is nearly impossible to confuse with any other self, and to generate that self through language into the bookstores and libraries of a very tangible and often financially successful universe.

That is not, however, to dismiss out of hand a narrative and metaphysical swerve in the last forty years or so that has placed our culture and the civilization that has preceded it under a radical interrogation that challenges all the premises of our humanist tradition. These strategies place in brackets what in Western culture we have considered our essence, and for us to continue in the humanist tradition we must confront and incorporate this examination. We must learn from it. But before we do, we must understand it.

## *POSTMODERNISM*

To this point, I have been using *postmodernism* and *fantasy* as though they were critically accepted terms about whose meaning most people would agree. Nothing could be less true. To present these notions as a settled body of ideas would be to lay myself open to charges of reductive misunderstanding. In fact, to present the ideas of *concept* and *periodization* without a handful of caveats would be critically naive. At best these are aesthetically pleasing patterns, kinds of shorthand by which critics refer to a number of discrete works which viewed from another perspective may admit innumerable exceptions and contradictions. We would be much more to the point if we kept in mind that, if at all, we should talk about postmoder*nisms* and fanta*sies*, just as it would be wise to speak of real*isms*, impressio*nisms*, and so forth. A narrative that discusses such abstractions must, as Jameson indicates, "like all narrative . . . generate the illusion of 'an imaginary resolution of real contradictions' " (Lyotard, xix).

Of all literary periods, the postmodern is still considered by critics most dubious. First, many see a continuity of literary concerns from the late nineteenth century to the present, and so view the attempt at creating a new term to describe a new set of concerns as premature at best. Next, the very word *postmodern* carries with it certain problems as a term. It connotes, as Ihab Hassan writes, a passing, a surpassing, perhaps even a suppressing, in a way that words like *classic, romantic,* and *expressionistic* do not. So even if there does exist a new set of concerns to discuss, there is a question of whether *postmodern* is the right word with which to discuss them. Hassan "half-antically" proposes as alternatives The Atomic Age, The Space Age, The Television Age, and finally the Age of Indetermanence (indeterminacy + immanence)—to which I might three-fourths antically add The Age of Absurdism, The Age of Silence, and The Age of Uncertainty—but in the end he realizes that,

> we come closer to the question of postmodernism itself by acknowledging the psychopolitics, if not the psychopathology, of academic life. Let us admit it: there is a will to power in nomenclature, as well as in people or texts. A new term opens for its proponents a space in language (*Dismemberment of Orpheus*, 261–62).

To phrase it slightly differently, there is a language game inherent in the idea of literary periods, and there is always something particularly exciting and even noble about wielding the terms of the avant-garde with bravado.

In the end, however, the affirmation or negation of such terms has less to do with their validity as descriptive words, and more to do with the often turbulent currents of academentia. With respect to this, there are two ways of viewing history—either as a series of disruptions or as a pattern of continuity. Whether or not the word *postmodernism* survives as a sign of cultural rupture or is subsumed under a broader term that assumes historical continuity, "the coining of such a word" at this time, at this place, as Allen Thiher argues, "is in itself a historical fact that will be of no small interest to future historians. They may prefer of course to dismiss the notion and reorganize the entire semantic space known as twentieth-century culture or post-Enlightenment literature in terms of some new classifications, some new language games. . . . [So] perhaps the twenty-second [century] will find for us a more euphonic name, though we shall, alas, take little comfort in it" (*Words in Reflection*, 227).

The coining to which Thiher refers occurred, according to Hassan (*Dismemberment of Orpheus*, 206–61), in Madrid, in 1934, with Federico de Onís' *Antología de la poesía española e hispano-americana*. Eight years later Dudley Fitts used the term *postmodernism* in his anthology of Latin American poetry, and in Arnold Toynbee's 1947 *A Study of History* the word is used to denote a period which began in 1875. In the summer of 1959 Irving Howe discusses the notion of postmodernism in an essay called "Mass Society and Postmodern Fiction." A year later Harry Levin approaches the term in his essay, "What Was Modernism?" Leslie Fiedler uses the word in his 1965 essay, "The New Mutants." Hassan (*Paracriticisms*, 17–28) himself first approaches the notion in his 1970 essay "Frontiers of Criticism: Metaphors of Silence," and, since the middle of the seventies, the term has come into wider and wider use. In his preface to the second edition of *The Dismemberment of Orpheus*, Hassan catalogs upwards of thirty works concerning postmodernism that date from 1971. And just in the last few years some excellent works have appeared on the subject, including those by Jean-François Lyotard, Christopher Butler, Alan Wilde, Charles Caramello, Allen Thiher, and a collection of essays edited by Harry Garvin.

Most of the discussions indicate that postmodernism may be thought of as a mode of consciousness that has gained prevalence since the Second World War, but that postmodern texts have existed for some time. Certainly one can discuss the postmodern impetus behind a text like *Tristram Shandy*, and Caramello has found the postmodern mind at work in such seemingly different texts as *Leaves of Grass* and *Moby-Dick*, while Thiher has touched on the postmodern turn in Cervantes and early Faulkner. That is, the complex of concerns that we have come to call postmodernism may find expression at any time in history, but they have found pervasive expression in the culture existing in the second half of the twentieth century.

Perhaps one way to approach the idea of *post*modernism is to explore the idea of modernism and outline its dominant features. Modernism was the prevalent cultural mode between the 1880's and the 1930's. It signals a reaction against the Victorian and naturalist modes. In other words, it is a reaction against the dominant assumptions of the nineteenth-century, postromantic sensibility, a reaction that negates the belief in materialism fostered by Marx, Darwin, and the scientific method based on Newtonian mechanics. It attacks the bourgeois mentality that gained power steadily through the eighteenth and nineteenth centuries; and it wars against the belief in naive optimism and metaphysical stability embodied in industrialization, urbanization, progress, and the image of the 1851 Crystal Palace. It is a response to the deep recognition that common terms of reference have been lost, and is the antithesis of a Thackeray, Dickens, or Tennyson.

The first traces of modernism coming into dominance can be found in a movement like Impressionism (its first exhibition was in 1874), with its breakdown of external line—the line of certainty—and with its emphasis on subjective perception. Symbolism (Moréas wrote the manifesto in 1886) may serve as an emblem of modern consciousness, with its stress on individual rather than communal reality, its antimaterialistic impulse, its development of private cosmologies, its belief in form-freeing and suggestive indirectness, its love of word symphonies rather than rational discourse, and its faith in a transcendent realm. Freud too feeds into the modern mind by fathering a movement (*The Interpretation of Dreams* appeared in 1900) that explores and delights in depth psychology. Planck's quantum mechanics (the first papers surfaced in 1900) shatters Newtonian cause and effect, and blows apart the belief that the universe is essentially stable. Einstein's theory of relativity (he published his first papers on it in 1905) destroys the Newtonian assumption of absolute time and space. Hassan, in one of his paracriticisms, lists seven concerns that cluster around the notion of modernism: urbanism, technologism, elitism, primitivism, eroticism, antinomianism, and experimentalism (*Paracriticisms*, 39–59).

In many ways postmodernism may be seen as continuing in the same vein as modernism; it too may be seen as a reaction against the dominant assumptions of the nineteenth century. But it is also a radicalization of that reaction. Whereas modernism developed a number of responses to the situation in which it found itself—responses that created a sense of coherence and ultimate order, as in the drive toward elitism, self-creation, and primitivism—postmodernism can no longer find any response adequate to the situation in which it finds itself, a situation consisting in the ultimate denaturalization of the planet and a deep belief in the imminent end of humanity (as I write, forty wars are being fought around the world by millions): a universe under physical and metaphysical erasure.

Postmodernism explores the impossibility of imposing a single determinant meaning on a text—and for the postmodernist, the world is a text. It explores this notion through the minimalism of a Barthesian degree zero writing (Kafka, Borges, Handke) all the way up through a maximalism of plurisignification (Sorrentino, Pynchon, Melville). So, in the end, the consumation of postmodern art is a kind of self-consumption, a decreation, either through an impulse toward silence, exhaustion of imagination, a sense of impotence and entropy, or through an impulse toward a cacophonous blast, a liberation of the imagination, a sense of out-of-control freeplay and diegesis. Peter Handke's prose exemplifies the first impulse, which through its redundancy of sentence structure, the announcement of void in a structure without complexity or individuality, where syntax bespeaks a vacuum and gives the lie to the idea of expression, moves toward what Roland Barthes calls "a style of absence which is almost an ideal absence of style" where "writing is . . . reduced to a sort of negative mood . . . a neutral or inert state of form" (*Writing Degree Zero*, 77).

A very different kind of deconstruction of language occurs in a writer like Thomas Pynchon. He suspends traditional laws of lexical and tonal consistency, and the resulting verbal anarchy triggers the downfall of his narrator's attempt at self-confident syntax. The lexical fields of mathematician, physicist, pop philosopher, breezy American, pervert, and so on, clash within his works to generate the linguistic equivalent of the pratfall where language slips on a wordy banana peel, stumbling over its own feet. The value of one language register—and, finally, language itself—is questioned by the existence of a multitude of others.

Whether a minimalist or maximalist strategy is employed, the result is the same: a radical skepticism of the capability of language to respond to the universe. This result may be seen through one of two optics, as Jacques Derrida intimates, either as "sad, *negative* . . . , guilty" or as "the joyous affirmation of the freeplay . . . without truth, without origin" (264). That is, many read postmodernism as that which adds up to Nothing, a frustrating and depressing nihilistic impetus to decompose, dismember, and defy interpretation. And alongside this essentially easy and negative reading there is another, an optic through which one can begin to see that all is *not* lost—or, more accurately, all *is* lost, and therein lies the delight. After all, absences may signal emptiness, but they also signal gaps that need to be filled, and that can be filled in an infinity of ways. Only when one realizes the notion of absence can one begin a trip into extended freeplay, a building and an unbuilding, a constructing and destructing, a misreading that gives birth to replenishment from exhaustion.

The problem inherent in both these readings, the negative and the positive, however, is that they see choice as something that exists along an either-or axis. And, as many of us intuit, either-or arguments usually are poor reflections of the complex world in that they reduce multiplicity to a binary. Perhaps, therefore, one may talk about yet a third optic, a kind of literary equivalent of Niels Bohr's idea of complementarity—the idea that through some shadow magic one must treat electrons not as *either* waves *or* particles, but as *both* waves *and* particles at the same time. Postmodernism, then, may be seen as both positive and negative. Indeed, as Charles Caramello suggests in *Silverless Mirrors*, at the same time the postmodern yearns for the stability that it has dismembered (think of the sadness and nostalgia of Beckett's Unnamable), it also joyously affirms its power to destroy because of the possibility it creates for regeneration (if Hamm and Clov cannot do much in *Endgame*, their not being able to do it is wonderfully, darkly funny).

The first traces of this mode of consciousness may be detected as long ago at least as *Tristram Shandy*, as I have mentioned, but it rose to dominance with the recognition of the Stalinist purges (1936–1938), the Spanish Civil War (1936–1939), World War II (fifty million killed), and Hiroshima (seventy thousand gone in a matter of minutes). Commercial television, developed during the forties, signals a purely passive relationship to art, the beginning of the quick-fix mind where complex and infinitely complicated events are reduced to simple equations. Commercial computers, developed in the fifties, become substitutes for thought and are seen to threaten the humanist sensibility. Abstract expressionism (de Kooning, Pollock, Kline) leaves the human form behind and begins the movement toward minimalism and maximalism. Sputnik, launched in 1957, signals the beginning of the space race, releases us from the planet, and underscores the smallness of the earth. Behaviorism, developed at the beginning of the century by Pavlov and Watson, comes to the fore after World War II and is seen to work against the Freudian myths of depth, concerning itself with the black box, with surfaces rather than a subterranean landscape. Quark physics (and the word *quark*, a nonsense sound, is taken from one of the first major postmodern texts, *Finnegans Wake*) seems to indicate that the building blocks of the universe hold an element of freeplay within themselves, whimsy, and even the idea of fictionality.

Whereas modernism may be read as the last heartbeats of Western humanism, postmodernism may be read as the first cries of posthumanism. George Steiner argues that with the postmodern "the house of classic humanism, the dream of reason which animated Western society, have largely broken down. Ideas of cultural development, of inherent rationality held since ancient Greece and still intensely valid in the utopian historicism of Marx and the stoic authoritarianism of Freud (both of them late outriders of Greco-Roman civilization) can no longer be asserted with much confidence" (ix). Alan Wilde indicates as much when he writes that acceptance is the dominant postmodern response. "Postmodern irony," he writes, "is suspensive: an indecision about the meanings or relations of things is matched by a willingness to live with uncertainty, to tolerate and, in some cases, to welcome a world seen as random and multiple, even, at times, absurd" (238). In the place of authority with its inherent belief in stability that existed in earlier movements, postmodernism shakily rests on what Raymond Federman calls *pla(y)gerism* (Caramello, 7), a kind of freeplay of suspension and acceptance, an acknowledgment that the universe is one of intertextuality where no one text has any more or less authority than any other.

Jean-François Lyotard stresses this aspect of postmodern consciousness when he defines modern as that which "legitimates itself with reference to a metadiscourse . . . making an explicit appeal to some grand narrative, such as the dialectics of Spirit, the hermeneutics of meaning, the emancipation of the rational or working subject, or the creation of wealth," and when he defines postmodern "as incredulity toward metanarratives. . . . The narrative function is losing its functors, its great hero, its great dangers, its goal" (xxiii–xxiv). In other words, the modern—and, in fact, each premodern movement as well—appealed to a metanarrative that bound the universe together, a metatext that told The Story about knowledge and culture—in the medieval world the metatext was God; in the neoclassical, Reason, and so on. But the postmodern appeals to no given metanarrative; the metatext no longer serves as a unifying force. Rather, the universe has become, for postmodern writers, one of plurisignification that strives against unification.

Hence, postmodernism decomposes two of the great unifying notions of humanism: the power of language to reflect and shape the world (see Thiher) and the power of consciousness to shape and recognize a self (see Caramello). But in spite of this decomposition, or perhaps because of it, a longing arises in the postmodern mind for what it has lost. As Caramello points out, "postmodern fiction may yearn for the book and the self that (its) 'writing' has dismembered" (35).

Hassan lists thirty-three traits of postmodernism, all of which in one way or another have to do with this notion of "dismembering," among which are antiform, play, chance, anarchy, exhaustion/silence, deconstruction, absence, dispersal, surface, misreading, mutant, polymorphous, schizophrenia, indeterminacy, and immanence. All of them register a culture of "ambiguity, discontinuity, heterodoxy, pluralism, randomness, revolt, perversion, deformation" (*Dismemberment of Orpheus*, 267–69). In the same paracriticism where he lists the seven concerns that cluster around modernism, Hassan lists seven that cluster around postmodernism: the city as death camp ("Anarchy and fragmentation everywhere. A new diversity or prelude to world totalitarianism? . . . Dionysus has entered the city"); runaway technology ("from genetic engineering and thought control to the conquest of space"); dehumanization ("Humanism yields to infrahumanism or posthumanism"); primitivism ("the post-existential ethos, psychedelics . . . the Dionysian ego . . . madness . . . animism and magic"); eroticism ("toward a new androgyny"); antinomianism ("Beyond alienation from the whole culture, acceptance of discreteness and discontinuity. . . . The widespread cult of apocalyptism, sometimes as renovation, sometimes as annihilation—often both"); and experimentalism

# Prelude

("Open, discontinuous, improvisational, indeterminate, or aleatory structures" [*Paracriticisms*, 39–59]).

All the above adds up to a "culture" in crisis. Virtually every mode of consciousness other than the postmodern believes in a transcendental signified—some ultimate realm of Truth, some eventual coherence, some *over there* that in the end helps define, articulate, unify, and make intelligible the *here*. The romantic mind, as exemplified by Blake, strives toward a completeness in which the contraries of innocence and experience participate. The realist mind (Flaubert, George Eliot, Zola) strives toward a perfect correspondence between word and world, believing in a realm where language is a crystalline mirror of communal reality. The expressionist mind (Munch, Kandinsky, van Gogh) strives toward an *over there* where art can be an act of purely unmediated expression of self. The surrealist mind (Breton, Dali, Aragon) strives toward a transcendent area that is somehow deeper and richer, more in tune with our fundamental impulses, than this one. Joyce believed in the omnipotence of language to order existence, Stevens in the Supreme Fiction, Hemingway in his Code, Eliot in the great Tradition, and so on.

But the postmodern mind has deconstructed the transcendental signified. It is one of the first modes of consciousness that appears to be for and against everything and nothing. Like Pynchon's *Gravity's Rainbow*, its impulse is to subvert the prevalence of whiteness within itself—that omnipresent colorlessness associated with the behavioristic investigations at The White Visitation, that "dead" blankness (268), that "enemy of color" (754), the image of closed systems, the stasis of certainty, the danger of the transcendental signified—while delighting in the possibility of the rainbow, plurality, multiplicity, mindless pleasures, the metaphysical equivalent of the Zone, where "all fences are down, one road as good as another . . . without elect, without preterite, without even nationality to fuck it up" (556).

So postmodernism is an attempt—at best paradoxical and at worst failed—to respond to contemporary experience, an experience that is continually beyond belief. Philip Roth, trying to come to terms with the role of art in current culture, says that the "writer in the middle of the 20th century has his hands full in trying to understand, and then describe, and then make credible, much of . . . reality. It stupefies, it sickens, it infuriates, and finally it is even a kind of embarrassment to one's own meagre imagination" (224). Our preconceptions of what constitutes the impossible are assaulted every day. In other words, postmodern art faces the problem of responding to a situation that is, literally, fantastic. No wonder, then, that fantasy becomes the vehicle for the postmodern consciousness. The fantastic becomes the realism our culture understands.

## *FANTASY*

The word derives from the Latin *phantasticus*, which in turn derives from the Greek *phantastikos*, a word that simply—and ambiguously—means that which is presented to the mind, made visible, visionary, unreal. The first traces of it in Western culture can be discovered in ancient myths, legends, and folklore. Its basic impetus is closely related to the ritual of carnival where misrule dominates and *Walpurgisnacht* briefly triumphs over *Alltäglichkeit*. Another mode that feeds into fantasy is Menippean satire, a mixed-prose mode that defies the demands of mimesis, and presents itself in dialectic form: character is secondary to ideas; answer is secondary to search; "meaning" and "conclusion" are refuted.

And yet throughout history fantasy has been considered somehow inferior to the mimetic mode. At the outset of her study, *In Defense of Fantasy*, Ann Swinfen feels obliged to note that "perhaps one of the most difficult aspects of undertaking a serious critical study of the fantasy novel results from the attitude of the majority of contemporary critics—an attitude which suggests that the so-called 'realist' mode of writing is somehow more profound, more morally committed, more involved with 'real' human concerns than a mode of writing which employs the marvellous" (10–11). At least since Aristotle's declaration that the essence of art is imitation, fantasy has been marginalized and identified as a relatively minor genre (see Hume's *Fantasy and Mimesis*). Attacks on it have thus always been popular, and have always been associated with a "high-brow" aesthetic. There seems to have always been a need to condemn or apologize for the fantastic, a need that is peculiarly ethnocentric, stemming from the deep belief in Western culture that "reality" is somehow morally "better" and aesthetically more "serious" than "fantasy," that the conscious is somehow objectively preferable to the unconscious.

Though fantasy has certainly had its defenders such as Sidney, Coleridge, Tolkien, and even E. M. Forster who in *Aspects of the Novel* claims that fantasy "cuts across" all literature "like a bar of light" (106), Plato, in *The Republic* (Book X), sees fantasy as an obstacle to knowledge an impediment that must be overcome—and so he advocates throwing out of his utopia all those who would release erotic, violent, mad, humorous, nightmarish, uncertain, female, and excessive impulses through art. Spenser throws his giant and unruly Phantastes into a cell in the House of Temperance so that they won't cause any trouble, and so that reason can rule supreme in *The Faerie Queene* (Book II, Canto 9, Stanza 50). Pope argues that too much fantasy is a bad thing, that goodness is "License repressed, and useful laws ordained" (line 682), in "An Essay on Criticism." Scott attacks the gothic fantasies of E. T. A. Hoffmann because they are psychologically suspect and in poor taste. Zola rings the death knell of fantasy when he writes in *The Experimental Novel* that "imagination no longer counts in the novel" (Stevick, 395). And even Robert Scholes, in his introduction to Tzvetan Todorov's seminal study, *The Fantastic: A Structural Approach to a Literary Genre*, cannot help adding that for him fantasy is "one of the humbler literary genres" (viii).

But, since the early seventies, a number of studies have demonstrated a strong interest in fantasy within the scholarly community. After Todorov's 1970 study come, most notably, ones by C. N. Manlove, Jean E. Kennard, Bruno Bettelheim, William Irwin, Eric Rabkin, Rosemary Jackson, Ann Swinfen, Kathryn Hume, and various editions by Roger Schlobin. Although such rigorous work on the idea of fantasy began over fifteen years ago, nothing like a communally accepted definition has yet surfaced.

Jorge Luis Borges suggests that at least one of the following four elements must be present in a narrative for it to be fantastic: (1) contamination of reality by dream; (2) a work of art within a work of art; (3) travel in time rather than in space; and (4) the presence of a doppelgänger (Monegal, 406). But clearly he makes no attempt to define his primary terms, such as "reality" and "dream," and one wonders in what way a work like *Hamlet*, with its play inside a play, should be considered a fantasy—except in the most general sense that, as Freud pointed out in "Creative Writers and Daydreaming," every writer creates a world of fantasy that he separates sharply from reality. Alejo Carpentier calls his brand of the fantastic magical realism and says that it "manifests itself unequivocally only when it derives from an unexpected alteration of reality . . . from an unaccustomed or singularly advantageous illumination of the unnoticed richness of reality" (Foster, 41), but again he does not define his basic terms. Kennard distinguishes between two types of fantasy, number and nightmare. Number (Heller, Barth, Vonnegut) is dehumanist in orientation; it is "anti-literature, anti-myth, destructive of form," and it "takes the reader systematically and logically towards nothing, towards the void, by breaking down one by one his expectations of realism." Nightmare (Burgess, Murdoch, Golding) is humanist in orientation; it is "basically a constructive form," and it moves "the reader towards a recognition of an all-inclusive world, a puzzle in which the pieces fit together. . . . towards infinity where there is mystery rather than void" (12–14). But Kennard goes little deeper than this interesting assertion, and allows terms like "fantasy" and "realism" to stand unqualified.

Others approach the idea of fantasy with slightly more rigor, many stressing the notion of "impossibility" that must be present in order for the mode to exist. Swinfen comments that "the essential ingredient of all fantasy is 'the marvellous', which will be regarded as anything outside normal space-time continuum of the everyday world" (5). Irwin defines fantasy as "a story based on and controlled by an overt violation of what is generally accepted as possibility" (4). Manlove agrees that for fantasy to exist there must be "a substantial and irreducible element of supernatural or impossible worlds, beings, or objects" (3). Here each hedges his or her argument by employing words like "everyday world," "generally accepted," "impossible worlds," as though such signifiers might hold the same signifieds for a biology major, an insurance salesman, and a literary critic.

Each attempt I have so far discussed defines the idea of fantasy epistemologically, as a way of perceiving "reality." Two more interesting definitions shift focus from epistemology to narratology, from the universe outside the text to the text itself. Rabkin reasons that "the truly fantastic occurs when the ground rules of a narrative are forced to make a 180° reversal, when prevailing perspectives are directly contradicted" (12). While this is more helpful than the previous definitions in doing away with the ethnocentric bias at the heart of most attempts to explain fantasy, it does not take into account a seemingly fantastic text like Kafka's *Metamorphosis* where the ground rules never turn since it *begins* with a fantastic occurrence. For Todorov, "the fantastic . . . lasts only as long as a certain hesitation" in the text and reader between the uncanny where "the laws of reality remain intact and permit an explanation of the phenomena described" and the marvelous where "new laws of nature must be entertained to account for the phenomena" (41). This hesitation, he claims, was experienced in its purest form in nineteenth-century fiction.

Clearly, however, Todorov still at times falls into the ethnocentric position of believing in the stability of terms like "laws of reality" and "laws of nature." Moreover, it is hard to understand why he should want to limit the fantastic moment to fictions from the last century, though of course the nineteenth century found a particularly powerful and ubiquitous outcropping of fantasy in the works of writers such as Poe, Goethe, Kleist, Brontë, Shelley, and Gogol.

Jackson takes Todorov's ideas and reshapes them slightly so that they both do not fall into ethnocentricism and do account for fantasies in and out of the nineteenth century. She defines fantasy as a mode of discourse. At one end of the continuum is the marvelous, at the other the mimetic (Todorov's uncanny). Hovering in between—sometimes nearer one end of the continuum, sometimes hovering nearer the other—exists the fantastic (33–37).

The marvelous is a mode of discourse employed by most fairy tales, romances, utopias, satires, supernatural tales, surrealist texts, and science fictions, a mode in which narrative events are backed by a coherent ideology (often Christian in romance, for instance, and humanist in utopia). Here narrative is shaped by an underlying meaning which is entirely independent of the particular story it expresses. The marvelous mode believes that human life is subject to immutable, universal truths. What results is a narrative that believes in the Truth of itself, a text that is sure of itself, with a godlike omniscience. Often the tone is impersonal, authoritative, certain, confident. The *here* of the text is the gateway to the *there*. This world leads to another. Often in the supraworld that is generated (*Yvain, The Divine Comedy, Star Wars*) goodness and nobility triumph, definitions of such terms are superfluous and redundant, and each speech act is declarative, self-assured, morally prescriptive, and ideologically true. Often the narrative situation has been set long ago and far away where times and places have ceased to disturb us. And often the conclusion is comic to the extent it implies an ultimate gathering together, reconciliation, an ultimately benevolent universe which is theological. In this way, the marvelous narrative is compensatory, looking back to a lost beautiful and often aristocratic moral and social hierarchy that was communally and teleologically meaningful.

If the marvelous mode concerns itself with a supraworld, with the *over there*, the mimetic mode at the other end of the continuum concerns itself primarily with what it believes to be this world, with the *here*. The mimetic or what Robbe-Grillet calls the Balzacian mode (Balzac, Flaubert, Howells) shares the Stendhalian belief that art is "a mirror carried along a high road. At one moment it reflects the blue skies, at another the mud and puddles at your feet" (*The Red and the Black*, 359). Like the marvelous, the mimetic is an essentially stable and compensatory mode in that it shapes experience into meaningful patterns. It believes in *a* world that is structured, coherent, and understandable both politically and psychologically. Indeed, the movement from the marvelous to the mimetic is also the movement from theology to politico-psychology. Whereas the marvelous signals the presence of the absolute and generic, the mimetic signals the presence of the pragmatic and particular. While the marvelous believes in immutable truth, the mimetic believes in the truth of everydayness and mutability. Impersonality evinces itself in both the marvelous and mimetic, but in the mimetic the ironic detachment and certainty are not those of a god but of a journalist. The mimetic mode does not believe in the aristocratic past, but in the bourgeois here and now: what does it cost? what color is it? how much does it weigh? exactly when did it happen? what did it feel like?

Hovering between the marvelous and the mimetic modes on our continuum floats fantasy, a mode that confounds and confuses the marvelous and the mimetic. It plays one mode off the other, creating a dialectic which refuses synthesis. Often fantasy begins in the realm of the mimetic, then disrupts it by introducing an element of the marvelous, the effect being to jam both marvelous and mimetic assumptions. In other words, fantasy is that stutter between two modes of discourse which generates textual instability, an ellipse of uncertainty. The stutter may last for a phrase, for a sentence, for a chapter, even for a novel, but its result is the banging together of the *here* and *there* so that neither the reader nor the protagonist knows quite where he is. That is, fantasy is a deconstructive mode of narrative.

What we are really dealing with here, then, is the question

of narrative "legality." Roger Caillois argues that fantasy is "a break in the acknowledged order, an irruption of the inadmissible within the changeless everyday legality" (Todorov, 26). Fantasy is a technique to dislocate, destabilize. In its pure form (Poe, Kafka, Pynchon) it is hostile toward anything static, rejecting any definitive version of " reality" or "truth." Hence, it is a mode that is hyper–self-reflexive, continually calling attention to itself in a way that purely mimetic or marvelous fiction does not. It announces itself as a linguistic game, and so Bessiére notes that "fantastic narrative is perhaps the most artificial and deliberate mode of literary narrative . . . it is constructed on the affirmation of emptiness" (Jackson, 37). Fantasy, then, is a mode concerned with absences, with what does not exist and what cannot be expressed, with nameless things and thingless names, with "a severance of connecting lines of meaning . . . a gap between signifier and signified" (38).

Following from this, fantasy's tendency, in its purest form, is to decompose unities of time, space, and character. Instead of the past, present, or future, only nowhen exists: Dali's clocks melt, Poe's characters wander in the town of Vondervotteimittiss where a devil storms the clock tower and pulls the belfry man by the nose, Robbe-Grillet asserts that

> it was absurd to suppose that in the novel *Jealousy* . . . there existed a clear and unambiguous order of events. . . . The narrative was on the contrary made in such a way that any attempt to reconstruct an external chronology would lead, sooner or later, to a series of contradictions, hence to an impasse (*For a New Novel*, 154).

Rather than the distinct relationships existing between objects in space, the animate dissolves into the inanimate, the *here* into *there*, the human into something other than human: so Daphne becomes a beautiful tree, a man named Molloy slowly comes apart until he is something Unnamable, the earth slowly blurs into the magical world of Tlön. Plot gains dominance over character so that the text centers on the question *what is happening to me?* rather than on *how do I feel?* or *what do I think?* In the marvelous mode, as both Northrop Frye and Richard Chase argue, characters are larger-than-life, ideal, abstract, and in symbolic relationship to each other. In the mimetic mode characters are equal-to-life, exist in a complex relationship to each other and society, are psychologically rich, and emotionally dense. In the fantastic mode, however, they are flat, insubstantial, unstable forms, neither abstract nor concrete. In a discourse of surfaces, identity is never fully established, the unity of self is abolished, the Balzacian belief in the fully-rounded character is radically deformed.

The language of the fantastic text takes the figurative literally. It refuses to take itself as poetry, which uses the figurative figuratively, so that "Donne's famous metaphor 'I am every dead thing,' for example, is literally realized in Mary Shelley's *Frankenstein*, and in Romero's *Night of the Living Dead*" (Jackson, 41). Instead of taking the word as metaphor, it takes the word as equation. In this way, the *as if* clause drops out of fantastic language. It is not *just as if I had turned into an axolotl* but *I am an axolotl.*

Saying that in a sense fantasy does not concern itself with psychology, for it does not believe in Balzacian character, is *not* to say psychology cannot help us better understand the mode. In fact, as Bellemin-Noël comments, "one could define fantastic literature as that in which the unconscious emerges" (Jackson, 62). Freud argues that the fantastic is the result of a projection of one's unconscious desires and fears into one's environment and onto other people. To do so, he says, is suddenly to make the familiar (one's conscious perceptions) unfamiliar (one's sudden perception of the unconscious). In this way, fantasy "is in reality nothing new or alien," he claims, "but something familiar and old—established in the mind and become alienated from it through a process of repression" (Jackson, 66). The fantastic is the sudden release of deeply repressed material.

Another way of saying this is, the fantastic reveals that which must be concealed so that one's internal and external experience may be comfortably known, so that one may get along day-to-day in the communal world. And the psychology of the fantastic need not be limited to the individual. It exists on the cultural level as well. The fantastic confronts civilization with the very forces it must repress in order for it to remain whole, functioning, and successful. Fantasy presents a culture with that which it cannot stand, possibilities of alternate universes: murder, homosexuality, sadism, and so forth. Thereby it explores the limits of civilization, decomposes humanist and religious sanctions concerning what is "proper," "decent," and "acceptable." It invites the individual to trespass, but it also allows a culture the possibility of vicarious fulfillment, of sublimation. Jackson writes:

> Fantastic literature points to or suggests the basis upon which cultural order rests, for it opens up, for a brief moment, on to disorder, on to illegality, on to that which lies outside the law, that which is outside the dominant value systems. The fantastic traces the unsaid and unseen of a culture (4).

Hence, the fantastic is a mode designed to surprise, to question, to put into doubt, to create anxiety, to make active, to make uncomfortable, to disgust, to repel, to rebel, to subvert, to pervert, to make ambiguous, to make discontinuous, to deform. It is a mode whose premise is a will to deconstruct.

## *POSTMODERN FANTASY*

Fantasy in its purest form—that strong, unstable hesitation between the mimetic and marvelous modes of discourse—arises, as Jackson argues, at times of excessive cultural unease, and so it is little wonder that pure fantasy has come to the fore in narrative since, roughly, the 1940s, and the rise of postmodernism. What I should like to do now is turn to eight writers who have come to be considered postmodern, and explore various aspects of their various fantasies, showing that at the intersection of postmodernism and fantasy pulses a deconstructive force—the autistic, though not necessarily nihilistic, push in what many have come to think of as that father of postmodern fantasy, Kafka, and two of his immediate sons, Borges and Robbe-Grillet; the linguistic crisis generated by the fantastic thrust in Beckett's texts; one of the most common techniques of fantasy literature, metamorphosis, as revealed in a postmodern work like Fuentes' *Aura*; contemporary fantasy's delight in and terror of epistemological uncertainty as it appears in Pynchon's *The Crying of Lot 49*; the tendency of postmodern fantastic fiction to generate narrative frustration in the reader, as exemplified by García Márquez' projects; and the metaphysics of absence that beats at the center of postmodern fantasy as shown in J. M. Coetzee's *Waiting for the Barbarians*.

Throughout, I shall emphasize what binds these texts together—the elements of postmodern fantasy. But it is easy enough to imagine other readers emphasizing different elements—the hyperrealism, for instance, of Robbe-Grillet's works, or the Faulknerian modernism of many by García Márquez—that would point to how dissimilar these artifacts are at some level. In each case, my approach will be eclectic, bringing to each text or textual complex those forces I feel most interestingly stir up its sediment. I realize, of course, that such stirring runs as much risk of creating mud as illumination, but I also realize that viewing a text through various optics allows a reader to gain a fuller picture of it. Interpretation need not be so much an exclusive project as an inclusive one. With this in mind, let us begin to diagnose fantastic autism.

# 2

# *Diagnosing Fantastic Autism: Kafka, Borges, and Robbe-Grillet*

> The house is the same size as the world; or rather, it is the world.
>
> Borges (*Labyrinths*, 139)

Franz Kafka, in many ways the primogenitor of postmodern fantasy in the twentieth century, was born in Prague on July 3, 1883, to a practical and overbearing father who established a prosperous business in ladies' garments. Kafka studied law at the German university from 1902 to 1906, when he found a job at The Workers' Accident Insurance Institute for the Kingdom of Bohemia and at the same time began suffering from weak lungs, headaches, constipation, and insomnia. He first fell in love with Felice Bauer, whom he almost married, then with Dora Dymant, whom he met at Müritz on the Baltic Sea and with whom he spent the last year of his life. In 1917 he discovered he had tuberculosis and on June 3, 1924, he died in a sanatorium outside Vienna, as the world moved toward its second massive fracture in the century.

His intertextual elder and often more devoted son, Jorge Luis Borges, was born in Buenos Aires on August 24, 1899, when Kafka was seven years old. Borges went to Europe, studied the Western tradition, completed his *baccalauréat* in Geneva when he was fifteen, and joined the Ultraist movement in Spain between 1919 and 1921. He returned to Buenos Aires to his prominent upperclass family of Spanish, Portugese, and English blood, taking an obscure post at a municipal library in 1938 where he was employed for nine unhappy years until Perón came to power and threatened him with the title of Poultry Inspector for Fairs and Exhibitions. Borges taught between 1946 and 1955, slowly going blind the while from a congenital eye defect. In 1957 he was elected director of the National Library and Professor of English Literature at the University of Buenos Aires, and four years later shared the International Publishers' Prize with Samuel Beckett. He died on June 14, 1986.

Borges' younger and often more prodigal intertextual brother, Alain Robbe-Grillet, was born on August 18, 1922. He entered the world two years before Kafka died outside Vienna, in Brest, France, as the son of an engineer, and ended up studying engineering himself, receiving his diploma in it. During World War II he worked as a deported laborer in a tank factory near Nuremberg. Afterward he returned to Paris and began surveying in the National Institute for Statistics in 1945. He traveled as a colonial engineer to Morocco, French Guiana, Martinique, and Guadeloupe between 1949 and 1951, when he decided to turn to writing.

Dreaming, fever states, delirium, nightmares, daydreams, and hallucinations pervade their fictions. The reader senses, not so much that he is living in a dream, as he does that he is living in the hypnagogic state—that state of semiconsciousness, of drowsiness and reverie experienced just as one is falling into dreams, where one floats away from an awareness of external "reality" and toward an awareness of internal "reality"; here the closed eye envisions a continuous procession of vivid and changing forms that are abstract in nature.

K. in *The Trial* (1925), for example, wanders through a claustrophobic universe of dim, winding staircases, wanders feverishly among the passageways at the law offices; finds himself in the painter Titorelli's gray room staring at variations (?) of the same landscape over and over again. Like K. in *The Castle* (1926), all Kafka's characters search for something through a world "hidden, veiled in mist and darkness" (3)—a twilight realm that exists between consciousness and unconsciousness.

Borges' universe, packed with mirrors and labyrinths, exists in a state of "fundamental vagueness" (*Ficciones* [1944] 19) like the compass from Tlön, "trembling faintly, just perceptibly, like a sleeping bird" (32), always about to trip into something else. It is a "blind and dizzy" (168) universe, where one world can gradually penetrate another, where everything and anything can be dreamed, where suddenly at night something can leap out at Juan Dalhmann in "The South" (1953), brush against his forehead—"a bat, a bird" (168)—and send him into delirium.

Robbe-Grillet's universe, as well, shimmers with the "indefinite light of a rainy landscape" (*The Voyeur* [1955] 4) filled with a "labyrinth of streets" (*The Erasers* [1953] 43), a "labyrinth of unlighted hallways" (*In the Labyrinth* [1959] 97), through which a psychotic Mathias, an unbalanced jealous husband, must wander. These are not the fantastic worlds that liberate consciousness so that it may sport among the freeplay of possibilities. Rather, they are worlds of phobia, neurosis, entrapment, and oppression whose topography, as Sartre notes in his essay on the fantastic, is filled with "labyrinths of corridors, doors and stairs that lead to nothing . . . signposts that lead to nothing . . . innumerable signs that line the road and mean nothing. In the 'topsy-turvy' world, the means is isolated and posed for its own sake" (66).

One conceives of the hypnagogic state only in isolation. One accomplishes it only in isolation. Such a state renders egocentricism complete. At best the fictions here maintain only a fragile awareness of any external "reality," and at their most excessive they are completely self-absorbed, completely removed from "the world," sharing a primary assumption that private "reality" dominates public, that the internal cosmos casts itself upon the external in order to reshape and redefine it. Such a thrust disintegrates communal plot (the public, the objective, the chronological, the external, the mimetic) and substitutes authorial plot (the private, the subjective, the anachronous, the internal, the imagined). In this way, literary fantasy becomes another word for literary autism.

Bettelheim, along with many others, argues that the enormous frustration, anxiety, and despair a child feels when he realizes he cannot completely control his world can, at moments, be utter defeat. Such frustration can be mediated through bursts of anger and temper tantrums which will usually abate when the child can imagine hope for the future. But such frustration can also be directed inward. "If a child is for some reason unable to imagine his future optimistically, arrest in development sets in," Bettelheim writes. "The extreme example of this can be found in the behavior of the child suffering from infantile autism" (*The Uses of Enchantment*, 125). Among the symptoms of this are "seclusiveness, loss of interest in surroundings, disturbances in emotional responses to people, emotional blunting, reversion to 'primitive' types of behavior, negativism, mannerisms, sensitivity to criticism, physical inactivity, repetitive movement, and idiosyncratic speech and thinking" (A *Psychological Approach to Abnormal Behavior*, 501). In the same way, the fictions of Kafka, Borges and Robbe-Grillet display—at one level or another—all the symptoms of texts charged with anxiety, frustration, and despair before the recognition that they cannot control the external cosmos, cannot partake of communal plot, cannot imagine hope for the future. In other words, they all display the literary analogue—and, of course, I should want to emphasize it is *only* an analogue—of autism.

Closed structures, locked doors, small stuffy rooms, mirrors, labyrinths, and narrow streets—all are imagistic registers of isolation, self-absorption, and the limits of the imagination. Even the very paragraphs with which Kafka's, Borges', and Robbe-Grillet's fictions are constructed are crowded with ambivalent facts, unable to open into dialogue, jammed against the possibility of white space, free space.

Gregor Samsa, for instance, in his parable of progressive autism, of ongoing contraction and withdrawal, exists in his shell, under a couch, behind a sheet, locked in a room, confined within his apartment, lost among the narrow winding streets of a city. The Hunger Artist confines himself to his cage. The man at the window is forever cut off from the imperial messenger who "is still forcing his way through chambers of the innermost palace." But "he will never get to the end of them; and even if he did, he would be no better off; he would have to fight his way down the stairs; and even if he did that, he would be no better off." After the stairs would come the courtyards. After the courtyards would come the outer palace which encloses the first. And beyond that would come more stairways, more courtyards, yet another palace, "and so on for thousands of years" (*The Penal Colony*, 159).

Borges suggests the same sense of disjunction between the self and "the world" when, in an interview at New York University in 1971, he commented, "I'm afraid there are no characters in my work. I'm afraid I'm the only character" (Newman and Kinzie, 399). In Borges' fiction, Baltasar Espinosa is in a dark house on a farm surrounded by floodwaters in the middle of a no-man's-land. The narrator of "Guayaquil" (1970) admits that "I can almost say I've never been outside this library" (*Doctor Brodie's Report* [1970] 103). At the end of "Tlön, Uqbar, Orbis Tertius" (1941), the narrator takes no notice of external "reality": "I go on revising, in the quiet days in the hotel Androgué, a tentative translation into Spanish, in the style of Quevedo, which I do not intend to see published, of Sir Thomas Browne's *Urn Burial*" (*Ficciones*, 35)—seclusive, uninterested in his surroundings, completely inactive, spinning out a language no one else can understand, since English, French, and Spanish will disappear after the Tlönic takeover.

Robbe-Grillet's Mathias and the husband-lover in *Jealousy* (1957) both fail to find release from their imaginations as well. They regress to primitive behavior, the former in the animalistic torture and murder of a thirteen-year-old girl, the latter in the possibly imagined car wreck and subsequent burning involving

A . . . and Franck. Both find themselves stuck in a web of repetitive movements, Mathias' psyche continually returning to the room where he either witnesses or partakes in the strangulation of a young girl kneeling by a doll, the jealous husband-lover's psyche continually returning to the centipede, an objective correlative of guilt and lust. Both Mathias and the jealous husband-lover are isolated from an external "world," the former on an island, the latter on a plantation. The doctor-narrator of *In the Labyrinth* never even leaves his room; instead, he spends his timelessness the same way Borges' narrator does in "Tlön, Uqbar, Orbis Tertius," spinning out imaginary scenes intended for no audience but himself.

Such an autistic impulse destroys communal, chronological, external time. Rather than taking place in time, Kafka's, Borges' and Robbe-Grillet's fictions take place in infinity, living in imaginary duration, in hypnagogic timelessness, Bergsonian *temps humain*, where the private universe holds off the ticking of the clock. Infinity transcends time and negates the possibility of future failure. In Kafka's projects, there exists the strange sense of time not passing. One of the Tlönic schools, Borges tells us, "has reached the point of denying time. It reasons that the present is undefined, that the future has no other reality than as present hope, that the past is no more than present memory" (*Ficciones*, 25). Like the old man in the general store at the close of "The South," all Borgesian fictions seem "outside time, situated in eternity" (172), and Robbe-Grillet says that time in his projects "seems to be cut off from its temporality. It no longer passes. It no longer completes anything" (*For a New Novel*, 155).

Any reader of these fantasies continually oscillates between wanting and needing to participate in the authorial "realities" of the texts that exist outside of time and place, on the one hand, and, on the other, wanting and needing to attain distance from the disorienting and destabilizing narratives with which she finds herself confronted. At every turn in the labyrinths she discovers the texts thwart her stock responses concerning narratability. Every sentence is filled with data, but someone like Borges seldom interprets the "clues" for his reader, and Kafka and Robbe-Grillet never do. Nothing works for the reader. Everything seems to work against her. In the Balzacian mode of the novel, Robbe-Grillet writes, "everything tended to impose the image of a stable, coherent, continuous, unequivocal, entirely decipherable universe. Since the intelligibility of the world was not even questioned, to tell a story did not raise a problem. The style of the novel could be innocent" (*For a New Novel*, 32). Now, however, literature has lost its innocence just as the universe has, Robbe-Grillet continues. It has become absolutely indecipherable and utterly unstable. In this way, the postmodern fantastic text becomes an act of aesthetic, metaphysical, and political revolution that is designed to throw the reader into epistemological discomfort.

Instead of "meaning," the reader confronts the literary equivalent of Freudian *Nachträglichkeit* or "deferredness of meaning," whereby the story almost makes sense, but not quite, and where the almost-having-meaning seems to promise that meaning has only been deferred temporarily. "Meaning" seems to exist, but it is just up the next flight of stairs, just through the next dark doorway, just on the next page. Often, therefore, the operative form of postmodern fantasy becomes the detective story which has been perverted through deferredness so that the center of the text comes into focus only through the characters' and reader's inability to achieve it. "Meaning" is contained in the failure to achieve "meaning."

Like sacred texts, those of Kafka, Borges, and Robbe-Grillet exist in order to be interpreted, and there is no limit to the possibilities of interpretation. Put positively, as Frank Kermode does, "the reader will find none of the gratification to be had from sham temporality, sham causality, falsely certain description, clear story. . . . The reader is not offered easy satisfaction, but a challenge to creative cooperation" (19). In other words, the reader becomes the ultimate protagonist of the story or storylessness. But put less positively, as Maurice Blanchot does in his seminal essay, "Reading Kafka," "the true reading remains impossible. Whoever reads Kafka is thus necessarily transformed into a liar, and not entirely into a liar" (Rolleston, 14). If the reader chooses to enter the text with the intent to discover "the true meaning," he instantly becomes a prevaricator of meaning. He may create his own "meaning," but he will never create the text's.

Kafka criticism is a parody of this notion of creative reading. The critics tell us that Kafka is both a religious thinker who strives toward an unattainable absolute, and a humanist who is only of this world which for him is devoid of meaning. Kafka's work is imbued with Freudian substructures, Kafka's work is antipsychological. Kafka's work is antibureaucratic and firmly set in Prague, Kafka's work takes place outside of political and geographical reality in the realm of myth. But, as Susan Sontag maintains, "it is always the case that interpretation of this type indicates a dissatisfaction (conscious or unconscious) with the work, a wish to replace it by something else" (10). If there is one "true" point about Kafka's—and by implication Borges' and Robbe-Grillet's—work, it is that his texts are wholly open to interpretation. Close to center, then, is Thomas M. Kavanagh's insight, that Kafka's project uses the form of a parable, and "the parable itself becomes a set of semes from which an infinite number of possible subsets can be successively generated" (Rolleston, 91).

Much Borges could be read as a commentary on Kafka commentary. In Tlön, for instance, all "works . . . invariably include thesis and antithesis, the strict pro and con of a theory. A book which does not include its opposite, or 'counter-book,' is considered incomplete" (*Ficciones*, 29). In Babel's library, every conceivable book exists, "everything which can be expressed, in all languages." The ramifications of this fact are frightening, because all possible "meaning" must therefore exist, "the faithful catalogue of the Library, thousands and thousands of false catalogues, a demonstration of the fallacy of these catalogues, a demonstration of the fallacy of the true catalogue" (83), and so on.

In Robbe-Grillet's postmodern fantasies, the reader is no better off. The first paragraph of *In the Labyrinth*, for example, switches point-of-view twice, and tells the reader that outside it is both rainy and sunny, cold and hot, windy and calm. Two pages further on the narrator describes the outline of an object on a table. It could be, we are told, a cross, a knife, a flower, or a human statuette—"or anything" (72). The narrator of that text describes whole scenes only to end with "No. It was something else" (122). Robbe-Grillet begins the novel with a strange preface, claiming that the "reality in question is a strictly material one; that is subject to no allegorical interpretation." The reader, he says, should not give the text "either more or less meaning than in his own life, or his own death" (28)! As Robbe-Grillet indicates in his essay "A Future for the Novel" (1956), the postmodern text may suggest many interpretations, may, "according to the preoccupations of each reader, accommodate all kinds of comment—psychological, psychiatric, religious, or political—" and yet its "indifference to these 'potentialities' will soon become apparent" (*For a New Novel*, 22). The horror for the reader is that if all meanings are possible, then none are.

Both reader and narrator, then, become protagonists and prevaricators who enter into creative cooperation in search for a "meaning" which does not and cannot exist. Another way of thinking of this is to say that they become players in a game whose goal seems to be "meaning," but which in fact is the game itself. Playing becomes everything, since winning is no longer a viable alternative.

One of the most fundamental notions in game-theory is that the game is essentially gratuitous, noninstrumental. Games, in other words, are ends in themselves. Play is a voluntary activity that creates order and hence "meaning" in a limited environment, and fantasy is a game that proceeds within the mind's playground. Usually in play, there are three kinds of players: (1) those who play by the rules; (2) those who cheat; (3) those spoilsports who refuse to play. But in postmodern fiction, there is also a fourth kind of player—he who wants very much to play, but does not know the rules. He has chosen to play in a game that goes on with or without him, a game which he cannot win. To this extent, he, as well, becomes an emblem of the reader of the texts.

K. in *The Trial*, for instance, relives the same scene over and over again in various forms—the trial itself, in which the hope of finding the message or verdict is continually undercut; he knows from the beginning, it seems, that he cannot win, but he chooses to play until he realizes that every assertion on his part is followed by its negation, at which time he succumbs to the other gamesters (the Law) and admits defeat (murder/suicide). The librarian of Babel knows from the start that he will never find the book of answers, the book of ultimate codes, and yet he plays out his melancholy life among the unending bookshelves. The jealous husband-lover will never be able to determine to what extent his paranoia concerning A . . . and Franck is justified, how much of a plot is working against him: does A . . . lean over simply to give Franck a drink, or is there something whispered between them? has there really been a breakdown that keeps the couple in the city over night, or is there an affair going on? is the native on the bridge only that, or is he some sort of spy for the couple? In each case, then, the character and the reader play out a failed game. They go on for as long as they can take it, and then they give up.

This giving up lies at the heart of Kafka's, Borges' and Robbe-Grillet's projects. In the end, nothing exists for the players except frustration, jammed hopes, false connections, misfired meaning, and, ultimately, despair. The narrator of "Investigations of a Dog" (1931) puts it this way: "People began to investigate after a fashion, to collect data. . . . And though the truth will not be discovered by such means—never can that stage be reached—yet they throw light on some of the profounder ramifications of falsehood" (*Selected Short Stories of Franz Kafka*, 225). Finally what one is left with is knowledge of a system of lies. The greatest sense of sadness here is not that all hope is finally evaporated, for that at least would make things certain, but that Kafka and the others find hope never quite succeeds in being condemned. There is always one more dim winding staircase to mount, one more scene of falsehood to confront, one more futile gesture to make. In *The Castle*, K. talks about his quest for "meaning" like this: "We have tried to get it by crying, by scratching, by tugging—just as a child tugs at the tablecloth, gaining nothing, but only bringing all the splendid things down on the floor and putting them out of its reach forever" (405). The futile gesture toward "meaning" is made again and again, thwarted again and again. As the priest in *The Trial* tells K., the scriptures may be unalterable, but "the comments often enough merely express the commentators' despair" (217).

In Borges, too, a sense of despair shimmers under his ostensibly puckish texts. Borges' narrators have nothing left but the disease of consciousness, and yet "there is no intellectual exercise which is not ultimately useless" (*Ficciones*, 53). Like Lonnrot in "Death and the Compass" (1942), many Borgesian characters are overwhelmed by coldness, "an impersonal, almost anonymous sadness" (*Ficciones*, 141). The librarian of Babel comments that he has spent all his life searching for the book of answers, for "it does not seem unlikely that on some shelf of the universe there lies a total book." His prayer is not that he may find it, but that "some man—even if only one man, and though it have been thousands of years ago!—may have examined and read it. . . . Let me be outraged and annihilated, but may Thy enormous Library be justified, for one instant, in one being" (*Ficciones*, 85–86). Utter defeat pervades the passage. Worse is the Borgesian notion that time is circular and repetitive, that the eternal situation is one of failure, that the situation the librarian finds himself in is ours, that we are condemned to live our lives, with minor variations, eternally, without being any wiser for it.

Robbe-Grillet's texts also are filled with failed meetings, unattained goals, lies. The jealous husband-lover stalks his house alone, obsessed with the idea of his wife's unfaithfulness. Wallas kills the man whose murder he is supposed to solve. A soldier wanders through a labyrinth of streets trying to find a man to whom to give a message. Often, Robbe-Grillet's landscapes are empty, "without a man, a woman, or even a child" (*In the Labyrinth*, 37), and, when they are populated, they are so by the feverish, the paranoid, the obsessed, the utterly static:

> An arm remains half raised, a mouth gapes, a head is tipped back; but tension has replaced movement, the features are contorted, the limbs stiffened, the smile has become a grimace, the impulse has lost its intention, and its meaning. There no longer remains, in their place, anything but excess, and strangeness, and death (90).

Texts fraught with such a deep feeling of failure invariably begin the entropic drift toward autistic silence. The game is futile, the center is absent, linguistic zero is present. With respect to this, it is interesting that neither Borges nor Robbe-Grillet can produce long fictions, and that the scant length of the latter is achieved only through frequent repetition of a few scenes. Kafka could only complete short stories. When he tried attaining any length, he could not finish what he began. In this way, all their postmodern fantasies tend toward the fragmentary, and the essence of the fragmentary form is mutilation, a sign of impossibility, of failed message.

No wonder, then, that Georg Bendemann writes to no one, that the imperial message reaches no one, the old manuscript is written to no one by the doomed survivor of a dying race. When Gregor Samsa tries speaking, there vibrates in his voice "a persistent horrible twittering squeak . . . that left words in their clear shape only for the first moment and then rose up reverberating round them to destroy their sense" (*The Penal Colony*, 70).

The same sort of communication fizzles pervades Borges' work, where, as in Robbe-Grillet, there is seldom dialogue; where Funes labors to create his own system of noncommunication, a system of enumeration by which every number would have a separate name; where in the great library of Babel "books . . . mean nothing" (*Ficciones*, 81). In his essay on John Wilkins, Borges quotes a passage by Chesterton which contains "the most lucid words ever written on the subject of language" for Borges:

> Man knows that there are in the soul tints more bewildering, more numberless, and more nameless than the colours of the autumn forests . . . yet he seriously believes that these things can every one of them, in all their tones and semi-tones, in all their blends and unions, be accurately represented by an arbitrary system of grunts and squeals. He believes that an ordinary stockbroker can really produce . . . noises which denote all the mysteries of memory and all the agonies of desire" (McMurray, 5).

The Borgesian subtext resonates with an overwhelming despair before the arbitrariness of language and its essential defectiveness for depicting the world, the same sort of despair before autistic language sputters that is embodied in Robbe-Grillet's work—those "tentative noises that have no meaning" (*In the Labyrinth*, 73). Like the dehumanistic fantasies of Kafka and Borges, Robbe-Grillet's narratives are themselves monologues that have nowhere to go, nothing to say, no reason to say, no real belief that anyone is listening, no message but messagelessness to communicate, linguistic misfirings filled with words that "are so faint that they disintegrate before [the speaker] has spoken them" so that "afterwards he even doubts whether he has actually pronounced them at all" (104)—a recognition that forms the starting point for Samuel Beckett's postmodern fantasies.

# ❦ 3 ❦

# I Stink, Therefore I (S)am: Functions, Fantasy, and Beckett

> All the Arts derive from
> This ur-act of making,
> Private to the artist:
> Makers' lives are spent
> Striving in their chosen
> Medium to produce a
> De-narcissus-ized-en-
>   -during excrement.
>
> Auden
> ("The Geography of the House")

Beckett was born to a Protestant middle-class family, he insists, on Good Friday, April 13, 1906, although his birth certificate gives the date as May 13. He began studying French and the piano when he was six, and attended school in Dublin and Ulster where he was a brilliant scholar and athlete. In 1926 he bicycled through the Loire Valley, and a year later earned his BA in French and Italian from Trinity College. He taught, briefly and painfully, and received his MA from Trinity in 1931—the same year he suffered his first breakdown. He wandered through England, France, and Germany between 1932 and 1936, settled in Paris in 1937, and shortly thereafter met James Joyce, his own version, in many ways, of Kafka's authoritarian father. When Beckett heard of the arrest of fellow resistance members in 1942 he fled to the Unoccupied Zone, where he remained until after the war, when he worked for a short time with the Red Cross in Saint Lô as an interpreter, storekeeper, and rat exterminator. Afterward, he settled near Rousillon with his wife, Suzanne, with whom he has lived since. In 1969 he received the Nobel Prize, though he did not show up to claim it. Joyce should have received it, he said, because Joyce "would have known what to do with it" (Bair, 608).

Throughout all those years he transformed the sacramental into the excremental and, by doing so, took the tradition established by creators like Duchamp, Miro, Dali, and Pollock to a postmodern extreme. His earliest literary output took the form of poetry, and even his earliest fantastic poems manifest this preoccupation with bodily functions. *Whoroscope* (1930), for instance, a piece based on Baillet's life of Descartes, takes the form of a monologue by the philosopher who likes his morning eggs hatched from eight to ten days. The monologue ponders the "stagnant murky blood" (*Collected Poems*, 2) of the eggs' fetuses, thereby making celestial knowledge obscene and life, as well as the history of the Western mind that Descartes began, abortive.

In *Echo's Bones* (1935), his first collection of poetry, Beckett repeatedly returns to his obsession. The titles "Sanies I" and "Sanies II"—Latin for "morbid discharge," "blood from a wound," "gore," "foam," "slaver"—intimate as much, as does "Enueg I," a poem that centers around the image of a young woman dying of cancer in a nursing home. The narrator of this poem sets out across Dublin, meditating on the woman's death, solitary and pained to the point where neutral objects of the city take on the weight of disease—the canal is "livid," the evening "stillborn." Beckett's cardinal images become excrement, blood, and putrefaction—those taboo images of a culture which his postmodern fantasies explore.

Throughout his fictions Beckett, who inherits Kafka's grim

comedy, fixates on these images. In *Murphy* (English 1938; French 1947), for instance, the protagonist dies violently when his garret blows up after someone below attempts flushing a toilet and accidentally pulls the wrong chain, releasing gas into Murphy's room, which explodes when the fumes come into contact with a candle there. Murphy leaves behind a note explaining that he wants his ashes flushed down the toilet in the Abbey Theatre, but the man entrusted with his remains gets sidetracked on his mission and ends up throwing what is left of Murphy at someone in a bar. Moran in *Molloy* (French 1951; English 1955) delights in brutalizing his thirteen-year-old son with painful enemas. The protagonist of *Malone Dies* (French 1951; English 1956), who spends his time making up stories about—among others—a boy named Saposcat (Greek for "wisdom" and "dung"), learns that "what matters is to eat and excrete. Dish and pot, dish and pot, these are the poles" (185). And for the posthuman Unnamable "all is killing and eating" (340). The only way it knows it is alive is because it knows its bodily functions are working, because—through some grotesque inversion of the Cartesian *cogito*—it stinks: "The flies vouch for me, if you like, but how far?" (341).

Such detailed representation of bodily functions in art, be it in the fantasies of Beckett or de Sade, the poetry of Swift or Auden, or the creations of Schön or Manzoni, is emblematic of a number of impulses. It stands for dark mirth at man's irrational half, an extreme parody of the realist impulse in the arts, a perverse parody of Freudian-Darwinian consciousness. It suggests, as Auden argues, "both the primal creative act . . . and the primal act of revolt and repudiation of the past" (Pops, 30). It signals a drive toward the extension of self in the universe, while at the same time a desecration of humanist environments—high art, bourgeois decorum, the body itself, the legality of the dominant culture, the religious artifact that connects us to the *there*: "we call it the arsehole and affect to despise it," Molloy says, "but is it not rather the true portal of our being" (80).

For Beckett in particular, there are a number of biographical reasons that help account for the variety of detailed accounts of bodily functions. At least since his days at Trinity College, and his first breakdown, he has suffered from a host of ailments, many of which appear to be psychosomatic: severe constipation, pleurisy, feelings of choking and suffocation, lung cancer, migraine headaches, bad cases of flu, aching joints that have kept him bedridden for days, cysts, boils, a chronic inability to empty his bladder, tremors, bad eyes, bad feet, bad teeth, a tumor in his jaw. So it is no surprise that one of his favorite French writers since his days at college should be the novelist and diarist Jules Renard. What impressed Beckett most about Renard, he said, was that Renard "always speaks so well about chewing and pissing and that kind of thing" (Bair, 119).

When asked how he arrived at the title of the short-story collection *Fizzles* (1976), Beckett said the pieces had been "farted out," and went on to define "fizzle" in accordance with the definition that appears in the *Oxford English Dictionary*: "1. The action of breaking wind quietly; the action of hissing or sputtering. 2. A failure or a fiasco" (Bair, 639). What Beckett has done, in other words, is to equate the process of writing with the process of flatulation. That is, he has equated language with bodily functions, has *reduced* language to just another bodily function.

Such equations appear frequently in Beckett's speech. When, for example, he tried to plug his own ideas into a Joycean grid of linguistics, he said he found himself "verbally constipated" (Bair, 94). When discussing his role as a writer he claimed that he "was doomed to spend the rest of [his] days digging up the detritus of [his] life and vomiting it out over and over again" (Bair, 352). For Beckett, as for Molloy, composition becomes "a link between me and the other excrement" (*Molloy, Malone Dies, The Unnamable*, 80)—painful, unclean, unpleasant. The act of communication becomes devalued, neutralized, diluted to the level of a quiet breaking of wind, a sound just this side of silence.

Hence, when comparing his work to that of Joyce, Beckett

comments: "The more Joyce knew the more he could. He's tending toward omniscience and omnipotence as an artist. I'm working with impotence, ignorance" (Fletcher and Spurling, 41). The gap between Joyce and Beckett, omniscience and ignorance, omnipotence and impotence, is the gap between modernism and postmodernism. While Joyce concerns himself with self-creation, with art-as-redeemer, with the journey toward surreality through the window of epiphany, Beckett concerns himself with self-destruction, with art-as-deconstructor, with the journey toward minimalism through the window of entropy and exhaustion. For him "the expression is that there is nothing to express, nothing with which to express, nothing from which to express, no power to express, no desire to express, along with the obligation to express" (17). The result, as Hugh Kenner notes, is fiction in which "all speech [is] a struggle with dying idioms, and human dignity, which asserts itself in speech, [is] an illusion readily swept away" (Kenner, 172). Beckett's postmodern fantasies are games that undo Games, languages that undo Languages, systems that undo Systems.

*Watt* (1953), for instance, is the story of progressive psychological and linguistic deterioration. Watt, whose name suggests misunderstanding, uncertainty, failed discourse, gets off a train for no particular reason, walks across town, and becomes the servant in the house of Mr. Knott, whose name signals negative meaning, the absence at the center of the text, a knot of complexity. Watt stays there for a timeless time, then another servant shows up to replace him, just as Watt himself took the place of a servant before him. Watt gets back on the train, travels to an insane asylum, and narrates his experiences out-of-order to another inmate named, tauntingly enough, Sam.

In the end, the story is an education in narrative and existential ignorance. Watt has learned nothing, has no idea where he is, who he is or why he is. He never answers the question inherent in his name. Nor does the reader learn anything about him save that he is always just on this side of psychological collapse, so that he desperately tries giving order to his world in the same way Borges' librarian or Robbe-Grillet's jealous husband-lover does—by cataloging, counting, figuring, doing his arithmetic, and imposing arbitrary fantasies on his environment in order to control it to some extent. This is the way of the Beckettian character from the narrator of *Murphy*, who gives the reader a full page of Celia's measurements, to the narrator of *The Lost Ones* (1972), who is more interested in the statistics comprising his huge cylinder than in the lost bodies who inhabit its niches and crevices. Watt figures the possible combinations of the words "sang," "cried," "stated" and "murmured" for half a page. He lists twelve possible reasons—though in the end he decides there could be more—why Mr. Knott ate his food the way he did. For ten tedious pages he analyzes how a dog and a bowl of food might be brought together. And all these machinations are in an attempt to impose his subjectivity on the external objectivity—"for since when were Watt's concerns with what things were, in reality?" (227).

Despite his effort, Watt's plans for coherence fail. "The world" refuses to respond, and so the protagonist withdraws from it in a move toward pure interiority, pure autism. He even for a while turns away from communal language, constructing his own system of fundamental sounds that seem to make perfect sense to him: "Dis yb dis, nem owt. Yad la, tin fo trap. Skin, skin, skin. Od su did ned taw? On. Taw ot klat tonk? On. Tonk ot kla taw? On. Tonk ta kool taw? On" (168). Such self-contained language reminds one of Witold Ostrowksi's definition of the prose that would have to form completely fantastic fiction—that kind of fiction which would "have to present creatures that are completely different from us and modes of existence and action with their space and time settings completely alien to us." Ostrowski argues that "to tell a story about them the writer would have to use a new, nonhuman language and then the story would be unintelligible, unimaginable" (63). The whole of *Watt*, of course, has not gone that far. But passages like the preceding certainly are realizations of Ostrowski's insight. For Watt, such prose is a rich creation, but for the reader it is simply an ugly expulsion.

Watt has created a language with its own game plan, but only Watt knows how to play.

The trilogy goes even farther in its movement from the external to the internal, organization to entropy, mobility to immobility, public language to private language. It marks the realization of the Beckettian protagonist in his purest form, one whose first traces stretch back at least to the short-story collection *More Pricks than Kicks* (1934) and Belacqua Shuah, whose name Beckett finds in Dante's *Purgatorio* (iv, 97–135). Belacqua, as Dante tells us, "shows himself more indolent than if sloth were his sister." He is notorious for his laziness and apathy, and must wait in the shadow of a rock until as many years have passed as he lived on earth. In Beckett's narrative—as in Coetzee's, as we shall see—all is waiting, sluggishness, and apathy in an ante-Purgatorial shadowland. A character named Molloy initiates a series of "protagonists" who fade farther and farther from the human—from Moran, Malone, MacMann and Mahood to Basil, Worm, and finally the Unnamable. The trilogy, then, is a story about metamorphosis, where the self continually teeters on the edge of becoming something less than self: a metamorphosis from one, through all the fractions, toward zero.

In the beginning there is Molloy, already static in his mother's room, unaware of who he is, how he got there, what has happened to his mother. The introductory paragraph is about five hundred words long. The second paragraph is about forty thousand, and tells of Molloy's long-ago attempt to reach his mother "who brought [him] into the world, through the hole in her arse if [his] memory is correct. First taste of shit" (16). Molloy sets off on his bicycle, slowly degenerating through the course of the narrative into a cripple dragging himself through the mud until he falls into a ditch, where apparently someone picks him up and brings him to the room he now inhabits.

Then a new narrator, Moran, takes up a new tale. Moran is some sort of detective, whom someone from the Pynchonesque Organization enlists to find Molloy. After receiving his communion without having properly fasted, and after abusing his son, he sets out, ends up killing a man, being abandoned by his son, and returning home in spring to an empty locked house. He is on crutches now.

Molloy and Moran are images of Ulysses-as-failure, detectives who search for self and homeland but find neither. They are, as Kenner notes, Cartesian centaurs—wandering minds perched atop "an intolerably defective machine" (119). Throughout, they question their quest, the possibility of knowledge and understanding:

> what do I know about then, now when the icy words hail down upon me, the icy meanings, and the world dies too, foully named. All I know is what the words know, and the dead things. . . . and truly it little matters what I say, this, this or that or any other thing (31–32).

Their enterprise, that is, is not only a physical journey. It is a journey through language and narrative as well. And both Molloy and Moran are painfully aware that words fail to fasten and hold, that they are only creating fantasies, voids, and not the past. They recognize that they are at the limit of selfhood and being.

The Beckettian narrative always constructs itself like that. It always gives the reader the impression that she has reached nothingness, and then shows her that she really has not done so at all. "From bad to worsen," writes the narrator of *Worstward Ho* (1983). "Try Worsen. From merely bad. Add—. Add? Never" (23). In *Godot* (French 1952; English 1954) Pozzo can still go blind in the second act, Lucky can still go dumb. In *Happy Days* (1961) Winnie can still lose the use of her hands and neck. And in the trilogy, the reader discovers that something else can always be taken away from the human. Molloy and Moran can become crippled. Malone cannot even crawl like his predecessors did. Mahood is just head and torso. Worm has barely that. The Unnamable is just a voice drifting in a void.

In *Malone Dies* the protagonist no longer even has a chance at externality, of open roads and forests and bicycles and crutches. Instead, he is bedridden. His only possessions are a notebook, a pencil, and a hooked stick by which he controls the skullspace of his room. His universe, as we have seen, is one of consumption and excretion—both physically and narratologically wherein he "eats" and "disgorges" his past, writing to introduce "a little variety into [his] decomposition" (254). Man is at a new border here—the one between the human and the excremental. By the end he crosses over. Malone dies, indicating first that the narrative may even continue after him. Let us "get on," he says, "with . . . my demise. . . . Then it will be all over with the Murphys, Merciers, Molloys, Morans and Malones, unless it goes on beyond the grave" (236).

Apparently this is just what occurs in *The Unnamable*, where a disembodied voice tries remembering if he is remembering a past or creating one, unable to place himself: "Where now? Who now? When now?" (291), so that "just at the moment when the world is assembled at last . . . all fades and disappears" (334). Here is Sartrean being without essence, the barest outlines of human form, where the pronoun reference breaks down before the reader and pulses in the shadowspace between masculine and neuter.

Just like Worm, then, the narrative here is limbless, blind, tattered, alone in blankness. *The Unnamable* is a discharge of prose devoid of subject by a "character" trying to play out a game of potential naming and controlling, whose rules he does not know: "there were three things, the inability to speak, the inability to be silent, and solitude" (396). Syntax and tense collapse: "These things I say, and shall say, if I can, are no longer, or are not yet, or never were, or never will be, or if they were, if they are, if they will be, were not here, are not here, will not be here, but elsewhere" (301). The text reflects a consciousness out of control, perhaps hallucinating, perhaps in a perpetual hypnagogic state. As such, its narrative becomes an analogy of bodily dysfunction, suggesting scatology by its presentation on the page—an outpouring of garbled sentences running messily down one page after another, where syntax becomes consumed only to be excreted in a more basic form, continually threatening the reader with its uncleanliness of form.

The last nine pages of the text are one "sentence"long, a series of words and phrases which semantically erase themselves until "they have carried me to the threshold of my story, before the door that opens on my story, that would surprise me, if it opens, it will be I, it will be the silence, where I am, I don't know, I'll never know, in the silence you don't know, you must go on, I can't go on, I'll go on" (414). This is literary suicide. The text does not end with the period. The white space that fills the rest of the page suggests the absence both the self and the text have become. About these last lines Beckett has said: "there's complete disintegration. No 'I,' no 'have,' no 'being,' no nominative, no accusative, no verb. There's no way to go on" (Bair, 400).

If, as Michel Foucault says, "the coming into being of the notion of 'author' constitutes the privileged moment of *individualization* in the history of ideas, knowledge, literature, philosophy, and the sciences," then Beckett's project constitutes the self-annihilation of the notion of "author" at the moment of dehumanization. Writing has become "a question of creating a space into which the writing subject constantly disappears," so that the writer "must assume the role of a dead man in the name of writing" (*Textual Strategies* 141–43). The phrases "I can't go on" and "I'll go on" function as grammatical antimatter and matter, cancelling out each other so that the last bit of discourse vanishes, negated by what comes before and after it— the equivalent of silence on the blank page. What the reader ends with is a text that voids itself both physiologically-scatologically and cosmologically-eschatologically.

After the excessive peristalsis of the trilogy, one finds only the constipated and dissipated prose of *Stories and Texts for Nothing* (1955), *How It Is* (French 1961; English 1964), *Ill Seen, Ill Said* (1981), and similar works, for all of which the dramaticule or nondrama *Breath* (1969) may serve as emblem. In print the whole play takes up less than a full page, in performance about thirty seconds. Here the audience finds dim light on a stage filled with rubbish, hears the sound of inhalation and sees the light becoming brighter, then hears the sound of exhalation and sees the light becoming dimmer again. Such a piece recalls the fragments of Kafka, Borges, and Robbe-Grillet, but with Beckett the mutilated form has been taken further, having been transformed into an aesthetically terminal remnant. Here we find only fundamental sounds, literally passings of wind. No one appears on stage. There is no presence. And perhaps again we have a piece from beyond the grave whose sounds reveal only absence. The essence of drama has been deformed. Such pieces announce the inability to achieve dialogue, the remorseless quaquaqua of Lucky's speech, analgous to the minimalist paintings of Rothko, Kelly, or Newman, to the silence of Cage.

Beckett's brand of autism also has great affinities—as I suggested at the outset of this chapter—with the work of Descartes, whom Beckett first read and researched in 1928 and 1929. In the Beckettian universe, Descartes stands for reason in Western culture, for the humanist belief that all sciences might one day be unified through a rational method and that the universe may thereby become utterly interpretable. In other words, Descartes stands for certainty, for epistemological clarity, for the Crystal Palace of the mind. Beckett takes Descartes and what he stands for and turns him upside down. How he does this is simple enough. From the *cogito* voiced in *Discourse*, Descartes derives two central and related doctrines. First, the "I" is a substance whose essence is to think. Second, this substance is distinct from any physical body it has, or virtually so, since for Descartes there seems to have been one point of contact, the pineal gland. While our consciousnesses can act in the world through our bodies, Descartes said, they cannot know them. Hence the comma between "I think" (the mind) and "therefore I am" (the body) stands for the pineal gland, a nexus, a hope of connection. But in Beckett's universe, that comma stands for a pause, for a gap, for the first stutter toward solipsism in Western culture.

Geulincx, a Flemish follower of Descartes whom Beckett studied in 1930, radicalized Descartes' notions concerning the *cogito* by taking them to their logical extreme. Unlike Descartes, Geulincx believed that the body and the mind were not connected at all, that at best they were only partially congruent. Hence for the Flemish follower there existed a mental world that was divorced from the physical one, which he believed just as real if unknowable as the mental one. For Geulincx, in other words, each person is stuck in himself. Each person moves through his mental life bounded by darkness, by a body-tight, Samsa-like shell. The only thing one can sometimes control is one's own mental state. Hence, one should not waste time and energy trying to manipulate the external world: hence Belacqua Shuah, and hence the narrator of *Murphy* commenting on Murphy's intellectual system: "Murphy felt himself split in two, a body and a mind. . . . his mind was a closed system, subject to no principle of change but its own, self-sufficient and impermeable to the vicissitudes of the body" (109).

All this adds up to the alienation from Cartesian reason, and thus from society, and thus from history itself. It adds up to an extreme dislocation from nature and from deity, a repudiation of humanist art and all it exemplifies, a subversion of the belief in form, shape, balance, symmetry, and order. It adds up to a scatological antilanguage that deconstructs public discourse. Beckett's narratives, through their foregrounding stasis, aphasia, inertia, exhaustion, and the vanishing point, accuse common speech and values and perceptions, and mark a new turn in Western culture—a refusal to persist, a refusal of heredity, evolution, and progress. In the end, then, they mark a literary and cultural boundary, since after Beckettian discourse the postmodern fantast must either give up completely or search for another route to the void. Carlos Fuentes, as we shall see next, decides on the latter.

# 4

# *Metamorphosis and Fuentes'* Aura

> "You should bring the cats in here."
> "The cats? What cats?"
> Fuentes (*Aura*, 53)

Although no clear historical pattern concerning the idea of metamorphosis exists, some sort of model does manifest itself in a very general way if one looks at the difference between premodern and postmodern metamorphoses in literature. Let us take a moment to examine an example from each category—one from Dante and one from Kafka—and then turn our attention to the uses of metamorphosis in Fuentes' novella.

In *The Inferno* (xiii, 22–45) Virgil and Dante make their way through the second ring of the seventh circle, a pathless and thorny wood filled with darkness and the screeches of the Harpies. This is the wasteland of the suicides, whom the church fathers from St. Augustine have put on par with murderers, since the self-slaughterer cuts short the length of life generously given by God. When Dante plucks a twig from a bush, the trunk cries out in pain and relates that he took his own life and that this is his punishment. That is, the self-killer has employed his godly gift, free-will, to deprive himself of that very gift. By doing so, he has destroyed that which separates him from mere plants, and so it is appropriate he be turned into a thorny bush—something closer to his essence than would be a human body. He has divorced himself from his body in an instant of intense and selfish passion. Dante has rendered that horrible moment eternal, enclosing the suicide in a subhuman form that will forever feel the pain and misery generated by the sacrilegious act.

Compare that transformation with Gregor Samsa's, certainly the most famous in twentieth-century literature. Gregor awakes one morning from uneasy dreams to find he has been metamorphosed into a giant insect. What is interesting is that Gregor is not particularly surprised by what has happened. If anything, he feels only a mild interest. At the same time he realizes what is happening to him is not a dream, he unemotionally scans his room, looks out the window for a while, and thinks about sleeping a little longer and forgetting what has just occurred. His only real problem appears to be that if he does not hurry, he will not make it to work on time.

Now just from the length of my own discourse on each of these passages, the differences between these two metamorphoses should begin to become evident. The text from Dante needs more language around it, needs more words to place it, to circumscribe it, to plug it into a grid. In other words, it needs a context: where are we? what has happened to these people? why has it happened? who did it? what does it mean? and so forth. The text from Kafka, on the other hand, refuses such language, rejects such placement. His discourse is briefer and it talks around the event, explaining what happened after the transformation. No amount of context will help interpret it. There are no valid questions to ask about it. In a word, then: for the suicide (as for Dante) things happen *for a reason*; for Gregor Samsa (as for Kafka) things *just happen*. With the first example, the context helps explain, locate, interpret. With the second there is no context; the reader is adrift; if she wishes the text to mean, she must create her own "meaning"; meanwhile, the text remains mute.

Following Irving Massey's and Harold Skulsky's lead, one may then begin to generalize about the two illustrations of metamorphosis. In the premodern transfiguration, the human body loses form. Or, more precisely, the soul separates from the human body without losing its individuality, and it enters something else. A posthumous body-substitution occurs, where the being generated is only partly congruent with his earthly identity. The process of transformation has filtered out the essence of a being and displayed it for all to see. This is important because whereas someone like Ovid presents metamorphosis as the human condition, someone like Dante presents metamorphosis as an exemplum, as the punishment of the damned or as the reward of the good. The premodern metamorphosis is by or for God or the gods, where the alien body serves as a means of edification for the victim or hero, as well as for the victim's or hero's fellows who may see in it an image of themselves. In short, it is a metamorphosis charged with certainty, reason, importance.

Just the opposite is the case with postmodern metamorphosis, where there no longer lingers a redemptive flavor, where no distinction is made between body and soul. In Gregor's metamorphosis, no teleological impetus evinces itself. There is no reason he has changed, no evidence of a guiding force behind the transformation, no explanation that aids the reader in solving the puzzle, because in Kafka's universe there is no puzzle. Rather, some people happen to change into insects while others happen not to. One cannot argue that Gregor's transfiguration is some sort of exemplum, some sort of punitive act that displays his essence for all to see, since no one and no thing transforms him, and since other "evil-doers" in the story (the boss, the father, the lodgers) remain unpunished, untransformed. In this way, the postmodern metamorphosis is one of chance, contingency, whim. It is unreasonable, unaccountable, uninterpretable. It carries with it no suggestion of what the reader is supposed to make of it, or, worse, it carries with it so many conflicting suggestions that each cancels out the next.

Though one may sketch in a premodern-postmodern pattern concerning metamorphosis, a number of general principles also hold constant over time. First—and again following Massey's lead—at least three major forms of metamorphosis exist. The most common is that from man into animal, plant, insect, or mineral, or the partial amalgamation of the human with one of these. This kind involves the movement from the human to subhuman. Second, people may metamorphose into other people, often becoming the antitheses of themselves (*The Strange Case of Dr. Jekyll and Mr. Hyde*), or they may metamorphose into parts of themselves (*The Nose*). Here the movement is from conscious to unconscious, from exterior to interior, from self to self-as-other. Third, a force outside the self can metamorphose into, or invade, the self ("Axolotl").

As the above indicate, metamorphosis usually is generated by a negative rather than positive force, although there are a number of exceptions to this rule (the good fairy godmother). Usually metamorphosis marks the conclusion of a process rather than a stage in evolution so that once it strikes it is unlikely to strike again. Such transformation often involves fear of engulfment, and often is violent, abrupt, ugly. Metamorphosis flies in the face of reason and repels consolation. Almost always there is some element of horror present since metamorphosis indicates that matters of life and death are beyond one's control. Often the change that comes about is irresistable, underscoring a lack of individual will and selfhood.

With these general principles in mind, we are ready to turn toward Fuentes and then his *Aura*. Carlos Fuentes was born in Mexico City, the setting for his novella, on November 11, 1928. He received his early education, though, in Washington, D.C., Santiago de Chile, Río de Janeiro, Buenos Aires, Montevideo, and Quito. Then he studied international law in Geneva, becoming perhaps one of the most westernized of the Latin American writers. Soon afterward he became a member of the Mexican delegation to the International Labor Organization, secretary of the Mexican Delegation to the International Law Commission of the United Nations, and cultural attaché to the Mexican

Embassy in Switzerland, all between 1950 and 1952. In 1954, the same year he published his first collection of short stories, he became assistant head of the press section in the Ministry of Foreign Affairs in Mexico. From 1955 to 1959 he served as assistant director of Cultural Dissemination and as head of Cultural Relations in Mexico. During the sixties he published extensively, and since then has served as fellow at the Woodrow Wilson International Center for Scholars in Washington, D.C., ambassador to France, and visiting professor at Cambridge, Barnard, Columbia, University of Pennsylvania, Princeton, Dartmouth, and others.

*Aura* has received relatively little attention and has remained virtually unknown in America until the last few years. Although Fuentes published it in 1962, it did not begin to acquire rigorous criticism until the first collection of criticism on the text appeared in 1982 (see Brody and Rossman, *Carlos Fuentes: A Critical View*).

There are several reasons for this apparent lag in critical attention. First, *Aura* was brought out the same year Fuentes published *The Death of Artemio Cruz*, a novel that overshadowed the shorter work because it was more massive, and seemingly more complicated and ambitious. Second, when the novella appeared it received bad press. Luis Harss and Barbara Dohmann, for instance, pass it off in a paragraph in their essay on Fuentes, and wonder why the writer ever attached so much importance to this "bit of literary inanity," this "mere fairy tale without suspense or illusion" where "even the writing seems lax and tenuous" and "everything works out too easily" (302). Third, and perhaps most important, there has been a general parochialism among American academics until the last ten years or so, wherein they have tended to stick with American and English works, and, if venturesome, have crept only as far as France and Germany, thereby failing to acknowledge the boom in Latin American literature which began in the forties with Borges' fiction.

I shall show that *Aura* is neither "a mere fairy tale" nor "a bit of literary inanity"—both prescriptive phrases that tell us more about the critics than the texts. Rather, it is a work charged with suspense, where *nothing* works out at the end. Fuentes himself holds up the novella—a highly amorphous literary form, and one that itself suggests metamorphosis, a transitional state between the universes of short story and novel—as one of his personal favorites, and recalls the inspiration for it came when he saw a picture of Carlotta, the wife of Maximilian, in the Chapultepec Castle Museum. The writer was impressed by how young and beautiful the empress of Mexico appeared. Some time later, however, he came across another picture of her. This time she was the insane Carlotta in her coffin, aged, and yet wearing the nightcap of a little girl. These two Carlottas, Fuentes says, became the young Aura and the ancient Consuelo, the double image of the same person (Brody and Rossman, 9).

But literary sources for the text abound as well. Among them are Chaucer's *Wife of Bath*, Pushkin's *Queen of Spades*, the gothic novel, the tales of Hoffmann and Poe, James' *Aspern Papers*, Stevenson's *Dr. Jekyll and Mr.Hyde*, and Faulkner's "A Rose for Emily." Even an earlier story by Fuentes himself, "Tlactocazine, the One from the Flemish Garden," which appears in his collection *The Masked Days* (1954 [see *Burnt Water*]), feeds into the novella. There, a young man falls under the spell of an ancient mansion. One day he strolls out into the garden that opens off the library and meets a mad old lady, Carlotta's ghost, from whom he can never escape.

In *Aura*, Felipe Montero, a young historian living in contemporary Mexico, answers a newspaper ad he feels has been directed specifically toward him. When he hunts down the address in the ad, he finds himself in the old section of the city in front of a large dark mansion owned by Consuelo Llorente who shares it with her niece, Aura, a beautiful young girl. Felipe's new job consists of editing French memoirs of General Llorente, the dead husband of the eccentric. Soon strange events begin happening. Nonetheless, he remains, attracted more and more to Aura. During his second night at the mansion the young girl appears in his bedroom and makes love to him. But soon Felipe notices she acts like some sort of automaton, as though she were the old woman's prisoner. Felipe continues editing the unfinished memoirs and there he discovers that Consuelo is a sorceress who has created Aura, an earlier version of herself. And while going through some photos in Consuelo's trunk, Felipe discovers that somehow he has become the General who died sixty years before—either through reincarnation, or some sort of magical metamorphosis. Consuelo tells Felipe she can only summon Aura's form for three days at a time, but by this point Felipe has lost his will to leave. He gives himself over to Consuelo who says she will try bringing Aura back again.

Even the novella's title suggests the possibility of metamorphosis which will occur on various textual strata. To examine the word "aura" is to begin a fall into the process of transfiguration. It is from the Latin meaning "breath," "breeze," "gentle wind," "upper world," "heaven." Over time it has also acquired the meaning of "zephyr"; a subtle emanation from any substance; a current of air caused by the discharge of electricity; the sensation, like cold air rising through the body toward the head, which occurs as a premonitory symptom of epilepsy, hysterics, and other altered states. It is, in other words, a shape that shifts meanings, blends meanings, changes their form.

A more pronounced metamorphosis takes place at the level of character. Put over-simply, Felipe becomes the General and the General becomes Felipe. Consuelo becomes Aura and Aura becomes Consuelo. Felipe, the young historian, is weak, passive, a studier of important events—"you like these jobs of careful research that don't include physical effort of going from one place to another or meeting people you don't want to meet" (29–31)—rather than a creator of them. In a way, he has always been a sort of voodoo puppet, a kind of automaton, worrying about what his students think of him, worrying about how much effort a simple step will take. Hence, he is like Aura, and by the end of the narrative he has turned into what he always was—a kind of pet who obeys, like the rabbit Consuelo has. When he answers the ad without much thought, he almost immediately gives himself, his will, up to the witch lurking in the old mansion: "This is Señor Montero," Consuelo tells Aura. "He's going to live with us." And Felipe repeats, droid-like, "Yes. I'm going to live with you" (27). During dinner he toys with a doll in the same way Consuelo toys with him, acting "mechanically," as though "hypnotized," with "sleep-walking movements" (99). In essence, then, he is a victim, the innocent youth of fairy tales who falls prey to the wicked witch.

Hence, he appears the antithesis of the General. It seems the only attribute he might share with Consuelo's dead husband is a perfect knowledge of French. Felipe appears insipid; the General strong. Felipe studies history; the General makes it. Felipe *reads* the memoirs in which the General *writes* about his impressions of Eugenia de Montijo, his visit with Napoleon the Little, his views on the Franco-Prussian war—writes about it all with a "martial rhetoric" with which he "harangues all men of honor." But this binary sense of personality turns out to be an illusion. In fact, the General too has fallen under Consuelo's spell. The reader knows him only through his overwrought language, not through his actions. He is more a man of apparently vapid letters than a soldier, and there is even the suggestion he may be impotent: "I have not been able to give you children, although you are so radiant with life. . . . We must reconcile ourselves. Is not my affection enough?" (131).

Consuelo and Aura, though the former usually stays in bed and the latter never leaves the mansion, are the truly active, aggressive, dominant characters. Consuelo seems to control Aura, and Aura controls Felipe—and, at one time, controlled the General. Only the two women, or perhaps different sides of the same woman, exhibit will, authority, and power. When Felipe first sees Consuelo, she is lying in bed in a large dark room, seemingly floating amidst a "galaxy of religious lights." The innocent historian reaches out his hand to greet her, but "you don't touch another hand, you touch the ears and thick fur of a creature that's chewing silently and steadily, looking up at you with its glowing red eyes" (15). The creature, it turns out, is a rabbit, a dual image of fecundity (which here is used ironically, since Consuelo and the General are anything but fecund, though Consuelo does have the ability to generate another being), and youthful lust. The scene of the old woman floating in a galaxy of religious lights is a subversion of a pious one. Consuelo is not the Virgin, but the Sorceress, the witch with a rabbit rather than a cat (though cats, the reader learns, also abound at the mansion). Later on she will ask Felipe with "a sort of croaking laugh": "Do you like animals?" The young man answers that he doesn't, and Consuelo continues: "They're good friends. Good companions. Above all when you're old and lonely" (81). This woman is a type of Circe, then, who will turn Felipe into her pet, a type of vampire ("I'd like to rest during the day," she says, "but come see me tonight" [63]) who feeds off the life of others.

Aura represents another part of the personality. She is pure enchantress. For Felipe, she is a window to another reality, though, as it turns out, not to a surreality, but a kind of living death, a *femme fatale*, a kind of Lolita-figure: "You stop holding your breath and run your hand through your dark, limp hair; you touch your fine profile [in the mirror], your lean cheeks; and when your breath hides your face again you're repeating her name: 'Aura' " (33). Felipe raises her name to the level of religious chant as his own identity blurs, becomes deformed, transformed. Here the mirror implies not only Felipe's self, but also Aura's, who is, as Felipe comments later on, "kept here like a mirror" (89). The child (though she grows increasingly old during the course of the narrative, appearing toward the end as a forty-year-old) is that into which Felipe looks, into which he falls, that in which he loses himself. In the narrative Felipe creates, Aura is Beatrice. In the larger narrative Fuentes composes, Aura is Delilah, a perversion of the holy:

> Aura, squatting on the bed, places an object against her closed thighs, caressing it, summoning you with her hand. She caresses that thin wafer, breaks it against her thighs,

oblivious of the crumbs that roll down her hips: she offers you half of the wafer and you take it, place it in your mouth at the same time she does, and swallow it with difficulty. Then you fall on Aura's naked body, you fall on her naked arms, which are stretched out from one side of the bed to the other like the arms of the crucifix hanging on the wall, the black Christ with scarlet silk wrapped around his thighs. . . . Aura opens up like an altar. . . . You hear her warm voice in your ear: "Will you love me forever?" "Forever, Aura. I'll love you forever." "Forever? Do you swear it?" "I swear it." "Even though I grow old? Even though I lose my beauty? Even though my hair turns white?" "Forever, my love, forever" (107–111).

In the universe of the ancient mansion, the Eucharist is perverted. Religious desire metamorphoses into sacrilegious lust. Though Felipe falls on Aura's naked body which is stretched out Christ-like, it is Aura who performs a subtle emotional rape of the historian. A Catholic ritual transfigures into a black mass celebrated on the altar of Aura's body—an altar, not of life and beauty, but of death and chaos. Aura is a sacrifice for Consuelo, Felipe one for Aura. It is as though youth feeds them both. The ritual of subversion takes place under a black Christ (the devil's Christ) with a scarlet silk (the color of corrupted love) wrapped about his thighs. After the ceremonial sacrifice, Felipe executes a debased catechism, swearing allegiance to the primal forces of the inhuman and the undead.

The distinctions between Felipe and the General, Consuelo and Aura, however, are not sharply drawn. They do not appear in the white light of reason. The line that separates Consuelo and Aura, for instance, is smeared at best. Consuelo creates Aura, but she also transfigures into her, and in a way is part of her—all at the same time. The exact relationship between these two remains perpetually unclear. At one point Felipe follows Aura through the house, down the spiral staircase, as the girl rings a bell "as if she were trying to wake up the whole asylum," but when he reaches the downstairs hallway, Aura has vanished. Then "the door of the old lady's bedroom opens behind you and you see a hand that reaches out from behind the partly-opened door, set a chamberpot in the hallway and disappear again, closing the door" (61). The implication may be that Aura has snuck into Consuelo's room. Or it may be that she has turned into the old woman. Or it may be that somehow she has ceased to exist for a moment. At another time, at dinner, a kind of fusion occurs: "You glance quickly from the aunt to the niece, but at that moment the Señora becomes motionless, and at the same moment Aura puts her knife on her plate and also becomes motionless, and you remember that the Señora put down her knife only a fraction of a second earlier" (69). Perhaps Consuelo is manipulating her puppet's gestures, but perhaps two minds have become one, perhaps Aura has suddenly transformed into a mirror.

Clearly, then, Consuelo-Aura and Felipe-General are personality-halves. But it is also possible that Felipe-General/Consuelo-Aura are all parts of one larger personality, perhaps that of a dreaming Felipe, or the Felipe who is creating the narrative we are reading. In any case, a process of continual transformation occurs, sometimes foregrounding one part of a psyche, sometimes foregrounding another.

In the Balzacian mode of discourse, one can define character as "the quality or uniqueness and persistence through changes . . . by virtue of which any person calls himself I and leading to the distinction among selves, as implied in such words as myself, yourself, himself, etc." (Chatman, 120–21). That is, Balzacian discourse believes in a unity of self, and privileges one character in particular. But in fantastic discourse such a belief is bracketed. Tidy definitions collapse. The text asks questions such as: what is "uniqueness"? what is "person"? what is "myself, yourself, himself, etc."? what is "a distinction among selves"? In Fuentes' postmodern fantasy, the subject of the narrative is doubled, perhaps even made plural, so that a duel arises, a game in which two—or here perhaps four, perhaps more—

people or parts of people try attaining possession of an object. In the game of *Aura*, the goal which is never attainable is selfhood.

This pervasive sense of questioning is indicated in the text at the level of imagery. The most abundant set of images cluster around lightness and darkness. Here the distinction between the two is not sharp. Instead, the universe of *Aura* floats in half-light, "grayish filtered light" (13). Color imagery also points to ambiguity. The most dominant color in the novella is green, first mentioned as Felipe is about to enter the mansion: "the cheap merchandise on sale along the street doesn't have any effect . . . on the greenish curtains that darken the windows" (9). A short time later it is picked up in Aura's "beautiful green eyes," in the green velvet curtains that hang in the parlor, in Aura's green dress. Traditionally, the color is associated with growth, youth, fertility, plenitude. While for Felipe it still carries such a charge, for Fuentes it becomes the color of Satan, prince of the world, the color of the deadly Latin American jungle.

As I have already suggested, religious imagery is perverted. Consuelo, whom Felipe comes upon kneeling before a wall filled with religious objects, appears, on closer inspection, "as if she were doing battle against the images you can make out as you tiptoe closer: Christ, the Virgin, St. Sebastian, St. Lucia, the Archangel Michael" (47). The old woman also performs mysterious sacrifices with cats and at one point Felipe comes across Aura in the kitchen "at the moment she's beheading a kid: the vapor rises from the open throat, the smell of spilt blood, the animal's glazed eyes, all give you nausea"; when he leaves to find Consuelo and talk to her about what has happened to Aura, he opens the door to her room and finds the old woman "standing behind a veil of lights, performing a ritual with empty air, one hand stretched out and clenched, as if holding something up, the other clasped around an invisible object, striking again and again at the same place" (91).

Not only the images change shape and meaning, but even

the objects, animals, and people who frequent the ancient house. When Felipe first arrives, he raps on the door with a knocker that looks like the head of a dog, but as he looks at it more closely it transforms into "the head of a canine foetus in a museum of natural science. It seems to be grinning at you" (11). As the historian walks toward a staircase, a woman's voice comes out of the darkness, or seems to do so; soon he is not so sure if he heard it at all (13). Elsewhere Felipe is told that a servant has been sent to pick up some things he left at his place, but neither he nor the reader ever sees the servant, and no one hears of him again. Felipe stumbles into a garden outside his room, but when he asks about it he is informed that the house does not have a garden (63). At the beginning of his stay, the young historian hears "the painful yowling of a number of cats" and when he wonders out loud about the noise Aura tells him that they have to keep cats because there are many rats in the old part of the city (37). Later, at night, however, when he asks Consuelo about it, she says: "The cats? What cats?" (53). Transformations such as these bring into being a world of perpetual shadows so that both Felipe and the reader enter a gap between what seems to be and what is.

Another way of discussing metamorphoses in the text is to approach the psychology of *Aura*, a story of the irruption of the unconscious into consciousness. At this stratum, Aura-Consuelo is the Other that rises up to invade Felipe-General's body and take him over. In this way, she is the dreadful Law of Kafka, the They of Pynchon. At the start, Felipe exists in a conscious, external universe of "the dates you must have on the tip of your tongue so that your sleepy pupils will respect you" (5–7). But from the moment he enters the ancient mansion in the old part of Mexico City, he moves deeper and deeper into an unconscious, internal universe of twilight, of timelessness, where he feels himself slipping into a "hypnotized stare that [he] can't control" (41). The journey Felipe embarks on is from reason to unreason, from lucidity to the hypnagogic state. Almost exactly halfway through the novella, the young historian falls asleep, and for the first time in years [he] dream[s], dream[s] of only one thing, of a fleshless hand that comes toward [him] with a bell, screaming that [he] should go away; and when that face with its empty eye-sockets comes close to [his], [he] wake[s] up with a muffled cry, sweating (75–77).

For the first time in years the subterranean surfaces, illegality breaks out. The young man wakes with a muffled cry to find Aura is caressing him, and he reaches out to find a key around her neck, the same key Consuelo was wearing around hers just a short time before (51). A question rises concerning this passage: is it possible that Felipe in fact does *not* wake up here, that his waking into Aura's arms is a continuation of his dream, that the second half of the novella only pretends to be a conscious report, when the fact is that all has transfigured into phantasmagoria, into a nightmare that will not end? If this is so, then the first half of the text represents the struggle between the conscious and unconscious, while the second half represents the triumph of the latter.

A journey into the unconscious is a Jungian night journey, an exploration of selfhood. When Felipe first reads the advertisement in the newspaper, he thinks "all that's missing is your name" (5). Such a recognition announces the text as a story about naming and identity. At its outset, Felipe understands nothing about himself. He skates on the surface of life as a bourgeois historian concerned with facts and dates, a person accustomed "to digging among yellowed documents" (5). But he digs through these useless manuscripts into important ones— those of the General, those that hold the clue to who he is. He moves from the edges of the new city toward the center of the old, into the past, into the self, into that archetypal myth dramatized at least as far back as Jonah's journey into the whale, where a solitary being undergoes profound metamorphosis involving a descent into darkness, into primitive sources, whereby a full integration of personality is possible. "You walk slowly," the narrator tells us early on, "trying to pick out the number

815 in the conglomeration of old colonial mansions, all them converted into repair shops, jewelry shops, shoe stores, drugstores. The numbers have been changed, painted over, confused" (9). Felipe has trespassed into a labyrinth, a form that stands for initiation and education as well as solitude and ambiguity.

Felipe's is a detective story, a search for self, but his education is perverted just as religion is perverted. While studying the General's memoirs, and the photographs in the trunk in Consuelo's room, Felipe finds his true self: "You stare and stare at the photographs, then hold them up to the skylight. You cover General Llorente's beard with your finger, and imagine him with black hair, and you only discover yourself: blurred, lost, forgotten, but you, you, you" (137). He recognizes his identity, but the recognition is horrible. What Felipe discovers is that he is no one, a dead man, not himself. His identity is the absence of identity.

Various narrative modes undergo transfiguration as well. For instance, the mimetic mode of discourse metamorphoses into what Fuentes calls the mythic, and what I have been discussing as the fantastic. This metamorphosis, Fuentes says, is the only alternative in literature that remains today, "a possibility of choosing this past, of leaving this past which is just history, vagrant history, in order to enter into a dialectic, which is to make history, and to fashion it out of myths" (Duran, 22). The mimetic belief in the external data of history is deconstructed by introducing an alternate belief in the marvelous charge of "choosing this past, of leaving this past which is just history." The dialectic, the superimposition of narrative modes, results in the creation of the fantastic. Felipe's universe at the outset of the text is clearly a mimetic one—that of the neat, bilingual teacher, a man who worries about catching buses. But even with the third sentence of the narrative, when we find that the ad "seems to be addressed to you and nobody else," a hesitation slips into Felipe's and the reader's world of order and stability.

Felipe then leaves the straight streets of the new city (the paths of mimesis) and plunges into the labyrinth of the old city (that which bends reason). As he raps at the door with the copper knocker, Felipe's world has begun to transform. The knocker abruptly is the infernal vision of Cerberus, the golem of the Kabalists, the register of witchcraft and black magic. The fumes from the streets are "unhealthy," the world of mimesis begins to fracture. When he realizes he is living in a fantastic universe, he desperately tries pulling himself back to the mimetic: "When you finish shaving you count the objects in your traveling case, the bottles and tubes which the servant you've never seen brought over from your boarding house: you murmur the names of these objects, touch them, read the contents and instructions, pronounce the names of the manufacturers, keeping to these objects in order to forget . . . the other one, the one without a name, without a label, without any rational consistency" (119). That is, he tries naming, tries labeling, tries like Beckett's Watt and Robbe-Grillet's husband-lover to make reasonable. But in the end he succumbs to the fantastic.

Another way of marking this narrative transformation is to discuss time in the text. Felipe moves from the present (the time of bus schedules and the new city) toward the past (the memoirs, the old city). Soon after he arrives, Felipe enters the process of rewriting the past, "of choosing this past, of leaving this past which is just history": "You spend all morning working on papers, copying out the passages you intend to keep, rewriting the ones you think are especially bad" (63). In this way, at first the present overtakes the past, and soon the past begins overtaking the present. And soon Felipe begins questioning time altogether, then loses all trace of it. "You can't make out the hands on your clock" (97), he says. And later: "You don't look at your watch again" (139).

At least two narrative devices suggest the pervasiveness of metamorphosis in the text—the use of "tu," and the use of French. Because the second-person point-of-view is uncommon in narrative, from the first word of the story the reader senses an imbalance, an unsteadiness in the discourse. "Tu" is a word that calls attention to itself in the narrative, and the opening phrase ("You're reading an advertisement") of the text calls attention to the very process of reading, and hence interpreting, and hence to the physicality of the text in the reader's hands. The "tu" refers to the "you" of the reader, pointing to the notion that the "real" narrator seems to be the reader himself, and the "you" of Felipe's memory or present consciousness-in-action, pointing to the notion that the narrator has become protagonist, that Felipe is both self and other, that he is both producer-of-script and actor-of-script. "Author" becomes a position to be filled by the reader.

The irruption of French into an ostensibly Spanish text also indicates the possibility of doubling, the presence of plural worlds, forms slipping into one another, epistemological unsteadiness. Reminiscent of Beckett's use of French-English, it stands for the inherent instability of language, becomes another kind of Borgesian self-repudiation, implying the inability of words to fix a world.

As Felipe is about to enter Consuelo's mansion, he looks up at the greenish curtains on the second level and notices someone drawing back from view. Later on, sitting at the dinner table, where four places have been set and yet only two people are eating, the narrator notes that "out of curiosity you try to read the label on the wine bottle, but the grime has obscured it" (39). Both images are emblematic for the process of reading *Aura*, a text whose center vanishes as we approach it, whose "meaning" continually undergoes transformation, whose label is covered with a fantastic grime so that clarity, reason, and order become impossibilities, and so that "once again you question your senses" (43).

To this extent—and I should not want to stretch the comparison, only intimate it—*Aura* is a text that has affinities with another postmodern movement, Op Art, an art of the sixties (that the visual arts affect Fuentes' style is common knowledge [Brody and Rossman, 193–99]) concerned with perceptual dynamics, retinal stimulation, the creation of optical effects, illusions, after-images, and continual and unsteady transformations. Explaining his optical dematerialization, Jesús-Rafäel Soto says "I wanted to incorporate the *process of transformation* in the work itself. Thus, as you watch, the pure *line* is transformed by optical illusion into pure *vibration*, the *material* into *energy*" (Gottlieb, 269). Such a statement could serve as well as a description of Fuentes' project.

All these fantastic artifacts liberate the gravity of mimesis and obliterate the stable shape of reason and consciousness. They force the reader-viewer to lose narrative control. She can no longer form a cogent story around the object in question—or, more precisely, the story she forms will be in the process of continual transformation, as will the object around which it takes shape. Fuentes has said he most depended on "the multilayered suggestivity of literary style" (Duran, 46) for his effect in *Aura*, and multilayered suggestivity assumes a world of radical flux, ambiguity, and uncertainty. This is the world of Thomas Pynchon, the next writer I should like to turn to, who picks up where Fuentes leaves off.

# ❦ 5 ❦

# *Pynchon's New Nature: Indeterminacy and* The Crying of Lot 49

> We all move in an Ellipse of Uncertainty, don't we?
> Pynchon (*Gravity's Rainbow*, 427)

Pynchon's penchant for science—particularly for the science of physics—is common knowledge and commonplace. He employs science as a metaphor, a guiding schema for his art, and an aesthetic model representing the phenomenal and spiritual worlds. For Wittgenstein, of whom Pynchon makes multiple mention in V. (258, 269, e.g.), the world is all that the case is, and for Pynchon the case is primarily one of disorder, heat-death, white noise, communication collapse, and existential blur. In criticism concerning Pynchon's use of science as metaphor, one most often finds discussed the concept of entropy, in which nature, according to the second law of thermodynamics, will reach a state of maximum disorganization and minimum available energy, at which time all change will cease. The next most commonly discussed scientific notion is that of white noise and distortion in information systems. Then comes Maxwell's Demon, the idea of nineteenth-century physicist James Clerk Maxwell, who posed the existence of a small intelligent being who can sort out swifter and slower molecules in a box divided into two compartments, thereby creating an inequality in energy (heat) without the expenditure of work. Little criticism has been devoted to Pynchon's use of relativity theory, which emphasizes the subjectivity of the observer.

In her article on Pynchon, Anne Mangel concludes that by using these concepts as guiding metaphors in his work, he "radically separates himself from earlier twentieth-century writers, like Yeats, Eliot, and Joyce.... The complex symbolic structures they created to encircle chaotic experience often resulted in the kinds of static, closed systems Pynchon is so wary of" (Levine and Leverenz, 99). In the end, the dense and intricate structures at work in modern writers can be filtered into a comprehensible system, but Pynchon's postmodern impulse is exactly the reverse of this. His understanding and use of the New Physics (although, of course, to some extent writers like Eliot and Joyce were familiar with such ideas) underlines the radical distinction between his fictional universes and that of the moderns. He revels in ultimate plurisignification, confusion, and indeterminacy.

In this chapter I want to add yet another idea from science that goes toward shaping the overall structure and the very narrative texture of Pynchon's (and in fact all the postmodern fantasts') output—the notion of uncertainty, a concept that has not been discussed with respect to Pynchon except in relation to *Gravity's Rainbow,* where he explicitly refers to Heisenberg's uncertainty principle (348). To this end, I should like to focus, after a brief discussion about the idea of uncertainty in the history of physics, on Pynchon's second novel, *The Crying of Lot 49* (1966).

Before beginning, however, I want to point out that indeterminacy is a particularly appropriate idea to talk about with respect to Pynchon, a writer who has metamorphosed his life into a myth of uncertainty. He does not allow any pictures of himself to be taken, and the Cornell University freshman register for his entering class (1953) holds a blank space rather than his photograph. Moreover, many documents concerning Pynchon's service in the Navy (1954–1957) were destroyed when the office in St. Louis which was carrying them burned after an explosion. His dossier at the Cornell College of Arts and Sciences has disappeared. And apparently his friends are as wary about talking of him as he is himself.

Mathew Winston in his article "The Quest for Pynchon" (Levine and Leverenz, 251–63) is able to sketch only the barest biography. The Pynchon family, which can be traced back to eleventh-century England, first came to the New World in 1630, and first entered literature as the Pyncheon family whose history Nathaniel Hawthorne traces in *The House of the Seven Gables* (1851). Hawthorne thought he had invented the name, but soon after publication he received two letters from the Pyncheons protesting the novel's appearance.

Thomas Ruggles Pynchon, Jr., the writer, was born May 8, 1937, in Glen Cove, Long Island, the son of Thomas Ruggles Pynchon, Sr., an industrial surveyor who worked for an engineering firm, and Katherine Frances Bennet Pynchon. When sixteen, he graduated from Oyster Bay High School. He was class salutatorian, and received an award for attaining the highest grades in English. In the fall of 1953, he went to Cornell to study engineering physics in which he read voraciously. At the end of his sophomore year, he entered the Navy, and in 1957 he returned to Cornell, refusing to join the honors program in spite of his excellent grades. He received his BA in June, 1959, with distinctions in all subjects; considered becoming a disc jockey; lived for a while in Greenwich Village; worked with Boeing in Seattle from 1960 to 1962; wrote V. in California and Mexico, published it in 1963, and received the William Faulkner Foundation award for best first novel. *The Crying* appeared three years later and won the Richard and Hilda Rosenthal Award of the National Institute of Arts and Letters. *Gravity's Rainbow*, originally titled *Mindless Pleasures*, was published in 1973, and shared the National Book Award with a collection of stories by Isaac

Bashevis Singer. In 1975 it won the Howells Medal of the National Institute of Arts and Letters, even though Pynchon declined, saying:

> The Howells Medal is a great honor, and, being gold, probably a good hedge against inflation too. But I don't want it. Please don't give me something I don't want. It makes the Academy look arbitrary and me look rude. . . . I know I should behave with more class, but there appears to be only one way to say no, and that's no."

To return to the idea of indeterminacy in physics: although it often appears, it has never been precisely defined. Instead, it has at least three different though related denotations: acausal behavior of physical processes; the unpredictable behavior of such processes; and the essential imprecision of measurement procedures.

The notion of uncertainty in atomic physics is by no means a new one. In fact, it stretches back to the beginnings of Western civilization. The earliest known thesis of uncertainty, which bears some slight resemblance to that found in New Physics, appears in Plato's *Timaeus* (ca. 348 B.C.), where the protagonist explains to Socrates that two levels of reality exist,

> that which always is and never becomes [and] that which is always becoming but never is. The one is apprehensible by intelligence with the aid of reasoning, being eternally the same, the other is the object of opinion and irrational sensation, coming to be and ceasing to be, but never fully real (Part III).

The Demiurge has created the phenomenal world after an eternal pattern, and only this perfect pattern can be spoken of with any certainty. The phenomenal world, the copy, can be articulated only in the language of uncertainties.

In *On the Nature of the Universe* (ca. 55 B.C.), Lucretius sets forth Epicurus' elaboration of Democritus' notion of atomic swerve, or *clinamen*. Although generally atoms travel straight down through an undisturbed void at equal speed, albeit with different weights, Lucretius notes,

> at quite indeterminate times and places they swerve ever so little from their course, just so much that you can call it a change of direction. If it were not for this swerve, everything would fall downwards like raindrops through the abyss of space. No collision would take place and no impact of atom on atom would be created (Book II).

If it were not for this small degree of uncertainty in the phenomenal world, nothing would ever happen, nothing would ever be created, and will could not logically exist. A perfectly determined world, a perfectly static universe—and Pynchon will echo this view—would be a dead world.

While ancient thought stressed, along with Ovid, that "nothing is constant in the whole world. Everything is in a state of flux, and comes into being as a transient appearance" (Book XV), medieval through early modern thought stressed a thoroughly rational prejudice governed by a theological faith. With the publication of Newton's *Principia* (1678), determinism began its movement toward dominance. The universe became predictable and static.

Not until the nineteenth century did such a view of "reality" begin to crumble. And not until 1892 was Charles Sanders Peirce able to conclude that chance is the basic factor in the universe. During the early 1920's questions arose concerning the limitations of measuring instruments in physics, and hence the growing improbability of attaining any sort of precise data about "the world." Both Erwin Schrödinger and Werner Heisenberg addressed themselves to the problem of indeterminacy, and when the latter attempted to describe the motion of wave-particles in terms of ordinary concepts like position and momentum he realized that the very act of observing a wave-packet disturbed it to such an extent that no accurate information could be gathered about it.

At least one quantum of energy had to be used to make an observation, Heisenberg imagined in what he called a "thought experiment," but the effect of this energy upon the particle was to disturb it so that it was impossible to correct for the disturbance. In other words, one could not know simultaneously to any desired accuracy the position and momentum of an object, no matter how good the instruments used and no matter how careful the procedures. If one knows the position of a particle, and not the momentum (i.e., mass and velocity), one cannot predict the particle's future position or momentum. Inversely, if one knows the momentum and not the position, it is equally impossible to know future position or momentum.

Niels Bohr, the third major figure in the evolution of the uncertainty principle, understood that the crux of the principle was, in essence, a Kierkegaardian belief in the irreconcilable dualism between thought and reality—reality understood is reality changed. To Laplace it had been evident that if we know the present we can predict the future, but the uncertainty principle asserts that we can know neither. For Heisenberg, the causality postulate became an empty statement.

> In view of the intimate connection between the statistical character of the quantum theory and the imprecision of all perception, it may be suggested that behind the statistical universe of perception there lies a hidden "real" world ruled by causality. Such a speculation seems to us—and we stress this with emphasis—useless and meaningless (Jammer 589).

The Platonic real world ruled by causality that exists as a pure pattern behind the phenomenal one became for Heisenberg an empty language game, and the intense discord between the Old and the New Physics became staggering.

William Barrett sums up this discovery by saying the uncertainty principle

> shows that there are essential limits to our ability to know and predict physical states of affairs, and opens up to us a glimpse of a nature that may at bottom be irrational and chaotic—at any rate, our knowledge of it is limited so that we cannot know this not to be the case (38).

A basic confusion results, then, about whether the universe is in essence chaotic or whether what we can say about it imposes inherent limits on our knowledge—that is, whether the fundamental problem is one of ontology or epistemology. And what more effective mode of discourse to employ when exploring this postmodern question than the fantastic?

In essence, the plotline of *The Crying* follows that of a detective story where a heroine-sleuth attempts to solve a mystery through the logical assembling and interpretation of palpable evidence. What better name is there, then, for the protagonist than "Oedipa," which harkens back to the first detective of them all? Oedipus the King seeks to reduce a complex and chaotic situation to one of simplicity and clarity. He seeks wisdom and thereby control over his experience. He struggles toward a center of illumination. Although the dazzling and terrible intensity of the illumination blinds him, he nonetheless attains the wisdom that he seeks and hence, to a certain degree at least, control of his experience. But the Frequentor of Tupperware Parties' Sphinx is one Pierce Inverarity, whose name intimates complication, puzzlement, and the inveracity at the core of the situation Oedipa is trying to pierce, and whose system, if it is a system, is the irruption of the inadmissible within the changeless legality of everydayness. His riddle is an enigmatic will which, it appears, is somehow tied up with the whole of the Tristero System.

*The Crying* seems charged with palpable evidence which can

be logically assembled and interpreted, although, as is common with a host of postmodern detective stories (those of Kafka and Robbe-Grillet, for example), the reader is never given enough evidence to know who did it, or what did it, and so he suspects everyone. Pynchon's example of the genre is a text of perplexities—I count a bewildering 266 question marks in a brief 138 pages—a text with a remarkably high frequency of mystery-words like "wonder," "chance," "understanding," "hieroglyphics," and "probability"; a text where the very structure of the language reflects the complex and puzzling situation in which Oedipa one day finds herself. At one point early on, for instance, the narrator comments that Mucho believed in cars,

> Maybe to excess: how could he not, seeing people poorer than him come in, Negro, Mexican, cracker, a parade seven days a week, bringing the most god-awful of trade-ins: motorized, metal extensions of themselves, of their families and what their whole lives must be like out there so naked for anybody, a stranger like himself to look at, frame cock-eyed, rusty underneath, fender repainted in a shade just off enough to depress the value, if not Mucho himself, inside smelling hopeless of children, supermarket booze, two sometimes three generations of cigarette smokers, or only of dust—and when the cars were swept out you had to look at the actual residue of these lives, and there was no way of telling what things had been truly refused (when so little he supposed came by that out of fear most of it had to be taken and kept) and what had simply (perhaps tragically) been lost: clipped coupons promising savings of 5 or 10 ¢, trading stamps, pink flyers advertising specials at the markets, butts, tooth-shy combs, rags of old underwear or dresses that already were period costumes, for wiping your own breath off the inside of a windshield so you could see whatever it was, a movie, a woman or a car you coveted, a cop who might pull you over just for a drill, all the bits and pieces coated uniformly, like a salad of de-

spair, in gray dressing of ash, condensed exhaust, dust, body wastes—it made him sick to look, but he had to look (4–5).

That is only one sentence, and sentences like it, which are not at all uncommon in the text, are as numerous and tangled as Inverarity's assets. It is a kind of archeological sentence, like those in Joyce's *Finnegans Wake*, Beckett's trilogy, and García Márquez' *Autumn of the Patriarch*, whose information density, parenthetical phrases within parenthetical phrases, epic and chaotic cataloging of a grotesquely decadent world, and convolutions and confusing syntax, all work to form a "salad of despair"; a complex bundle of meaning that indicates the complex universe Oedipa inhabits, and jams the reader's sensibilities. Just as Oedipa feels an information overload before such a complex and uncertain "reality," so too does the reader feel an information overload before such complex and uncertain sentences.

This density of syntax points as well to Pynchon's departure from the plotline of a simple detective story. Although *The Crying* begins with a relatively simple situation that appears imminently solvable, events soon slip from Oedipa's control, and, rather than a movement toward resolution and clarity, one finds a movement toward irresolution and indeterminacy. The simple becomes intricate, the precise knotty, the transparent opaque, and clues become unimportant because neither they nor any kind of deduction can begin to lead one toward any solution. In this way, Pynchon reverses the plotline of a detective story. The movement becomes one from certainty to uncertainty. It is not clarity and Truth that lie as the grail at the end of Oedipa's quest, but only the world itself.

By the end of the second chapter, the sophomoric and throwaway humor of name-gags like those in the law firm of Warpe, Wistful, Kubitschek and McMingus, Dr. Hilarius, and radio station KCUF, the cartoon characters of Manny Di Presso, Baby Igor and the rock group the Paranoids, the idea of the Vivaldi Kazoo Concerto or songs like "I Want to Kiss Your Feet" all burn away before the dark illumination that the game is real, that whimsy is nowhere to be found, and the universe is filled with a horrible possibility. In place of the sophomoric comedy we see a postmodern Joseph K., no longer searching for a center in *The Trial*, but scrambling through the matrices of a great digital computer.

What Oedipa finds is that she exists in a positionless world, a universe in which the center shifts, a cosmos governed by "magic, anonymous and malignant, visited on her from outside and for no reason at all" (11). The Tristero System is a projection of terror, the fear of metamorphosis and fusion, that silenced area in the culture. Existence for Oedipa contains "a hieroglyphic sense of concealed meaning, of an intent to communicate," where "a revelation . . . trembled just past the threshold of understanding" (13). Although for her, meaning always seems near—as for Kafka's protagonists, it is always just around the corner, just up the next flight of stairs—it never materializes. As she approaches one seeming center of meaning, it shifts or vanishes altogether, and she is confronted by another. She finds a kind of perverse sustenance through her quest. Her world thereby echoes that of another Pynchon protagonist, Stencil in *V.*, who realizes:

> Finding [V.], what then? Only that what love there was to Stencil had become directed entirely inward, toward this acquired sense of animateness. . . . To sustain it he had to hunt V.: but if he should find her, where else would there be to go but back into half-consciousness? He tried not to think, therefore, about any end to the search. Approach and avoid (44).

The quest is everything, the resolution superfluous.

Shifts in the center start small. Pierce, for instance, on the phone calls Oedipa "Margo" rather than using her real name. Metzger, also known as Baby Igor, notes that "our beauty . . . lies in this extended capacity for convolution. . . . Raymond

Burr is an actor, impersonating a lawyer, who in front of a jury becomes an actor. Me, I'm a former actor who became a lawyer" (20). The Peter Pinquid Society is so far right it appears left. As one approaches an object, its significance changes.

So after the first mail-call at The Scope, it seems clear that the answer to W.A.S.T.E. lies somewhere in the brilliant halls of Yoyodyne, but soon that possibility vanishes. At first the G. I. bones at the bottom of Lago di Pieta seem to be significant, but soon just what significance they might have becomes unclear. Although readers have bravely wrestled with the convoluted plot of *The Courier's Tragedy*, it seems clear that the very fact of the convolutions is what is important, and not the play per se. Although Randolph Driblette at first appears to offer some center of hope and light, by the end of the novel he has walked into the Pacific Ocean one night, thereby taking any meaning with him. When Oedipa comes upon Stanley Koteks somewhere in the labyrinth of Yoyodyne, she finds him doodling something that looks like a post horn, so when he tells her about the Nefastis Machine, Oedipa believes that that too must hold some significance, but nothing comes of it either. Old Mr. Thoth at Vesperhaven House tells Oedipa the story of the false Indians, and shows her the ring with the W.A.S.T.E. symbol on it, and then vanishes from the text. Genghis Cohen, the philatelist, appears to help Oedipa solve the mystery of Tristero, but at the crying he shows up mysteriously and starts making excuses.

At one point Oedipa stops to wonder whether

> at the end of this (if it were supposed to end), she too might not be left with only compiled memories of clues, announcements, intimations, but never the central truth itself, which must somehow be too bright for her memory to hold; which must always blaze out, destroying its own messages irreversibly, leaving an overexposed blank when the ordinary world comes back (69).

But in her universe there exists no central truth. Only for the protagonist of the Sophoclean drama could the central truth be too bright for the memory to hold. Only in someone else's narrative could there exist a central truth. At the heart of this text, however, beats only an absence, a waiting for "truth" that will not be fulfilled. As it is with regard to the uncertainty principle, so it is with regard to Oedipa's quest—the more she tries to focus on one element in the equation of her situation, the more uncertain she becomes of everything else. The best she is left with is a system of chance. One thinks of that crazy can flying around the bathroom of the Echo Courts Motel while Oedipa and Metzger huddle together on the floor, unable to know where it may hit or whither it may be going or when it might cease its absurd flight.

Of course the world presents Oedipa with a number of answers, approximations of "truth," but each one reveals itself in the end as either absurd or useless. Dr. Hilarius, for example, tries to control reality by making faces at it. Jesús Arabal talks about miracles and political revolutions while he sits exiled in some greasy spoon restaurant somewhere in California. For Mucho, the world makes perfect sense, but that is only because his brain has been fried with LSD. Pierce himself suggests that one should "keep it bouncing . . . that's all the secret, keep it bouncing" (134), but what kind of "truth" is that for a person like Oedipa, whose only impulses seem to be the finding of meaning and accumulating clues? As Driblette warns, "you can put together clues, develop a thesis, or several, about why characters reacted to the Trystero possibility the way they did, why the assassins came on, why the black costumes. You could waste your life that way and never touched the truth" (56). This is exactly what she does. As with Oedipus, Oedipa must search for meaning at the risk that that meaning may turn on her.

As with the characters in Ovid's *Metamorphoses*, Oedipa's universe teeters on the edge of an infinite number of others. As with Democritus' physical world, Oedipa's "reality" is composed of subtle swerves and shifts that lead her always away from a center and toward a randomness. As with Plato, the phenomenal universe of Oedipa's is always one of becoming, never one of being. There exists the possibility for a more real and meaningfully determined universe behind this one, but, unlike Plato, for Oedipa that ordered universe—that static, closed system of which Pynchon is so wary—would be malevolent and brutally anonymous. Everything in the world, then, has existence, not in fact and clarity, but in possibility:

> Either you have stumbled, without the aid of LSD or other indole alkaloids, onto a secret richness and concealed density of dream; onto a network by which X number of Americans are truly communicating whilst reserving their lies, recitations of routine, arid betrayals of spiritual poverty, for the official government delivery system; maybe even onto a real alternative to the exitlessness, to the absence of surprise in life, that harrows the head of everybody American you know, and you too, sweetie. Or you are hallucinating it. Or a plot has been mounted against you, so expensive and elaborate . . . so labyrinthine that it must have meaning beyond just a practical joke. Or you are fantasying some such plot, in which case you are a nut, Oedipa, out of your skull (128).

Or, as she puts it several pages later:

> it was now like walking among the matrices of a great digital computer, the zeroes and ones twinned above, hanging like balanced mobiles right and left, ahead, thick, maybe endless. Behind hieroglyphic streets there would either be transcendent meaning, or only earth. . . . Ones and zeroes. . . . Another mode of meaning behind the obvious, or none (136–137).

Oedipa, that is, reduces her universe to a system of either/or possibilities for which no precise truth-value can ever be determined. Her formula is easy, and utterly disturbing: either everything makes sense, or nothing makes sense. The distance between one and zero is on the one hand fractional, on the other infinite. If everything makes sense, Oedipa is a pawn in a ghastly and crazy plot. If nothing makes sense, Oedipa is floating in a ghastly and crazy world. The more she attempts pinpointing the validity of one side of the proposition, the more the other side reveals itself as possibly being the case.

Nor is Oedipa the only one reduced to such continual epistemological uncertainty. Because of the intrinsic positionlessness of the text, the reader too finds herself stumbling among the matrices of a great digital computer. When teaching *The Crying*, I find my students can put up with the absurdity of the first two chapters because the text does not seem to take itself seriously. With the introduction of the Tristero System in chapter three, however, hesitation, frustration, and even resentment build. My students find themselves in a world seemingly filled to bursting with palpable evidence, and they sense that their job as readers is the same as it would be in the case of a book by Arthur Conan Doyle or Agatha Christie—to assemble information in order to attain a clear and understandable whole. As the textual centers begin shifting, "truth" dissolves, and as an opaque haze settles on the words, anger mounts. Students feel resentment in the face of such information density, false leads, the dearth of any real ones, the fiendish plot of *The Courier's Tragedy*, the compact tales of Peter Pinguid, or the bones on the bottom of the lake. Such relentless inconclusion is enough to frustrate any reader. The narrator of *Gravity's Rainbow* points to as much when once he condescendingly interrupts his narrative to say, "You will want cause and effect. All right" (663). What he gives, and what the narrator of *The Crying* gives, is just the opposite. So again, the reader confronts a postmodern fantasy that demands to be interpreted and understood on the one hand, while, on the other, deliberately refusing interpretation and understanding.

As James Nohrnberg points out in his article on Pynchon, one convention of satire—from *Satyricon* (ca. 66 A.D.) to *Dead Souls* (1842) and beyond—is the lost or recovered manuscript that exists in fragmentary or unfinished form. Even the satires that do not make use of this convention make use of a related one, whereby—as in Rabelais or Sterne—the work does not conclude at all conclusively. In the end, "the reader's sense of being defrauded of what becomes a consistent or cherished illusion actually signals the fulfillment of the satiric design" (Mendelson, 161). Perhaps this is the final and most radical uncertainty concerning *The Crying*. Just like the old Hollywood cliff-hangers, Pynchon's text breaks off at the climatic moment, the moment of "truth," as does Beckett's *The Unnamable* which ends at "the threshold of my story, before the door that opens on my story" (414), and thereby completely frustrates the reader's expectations, jams all progress forward, thwarts any sense of wholeness, and thrusts the reader into a web of perplexity, distraction, and incertitude. At very best, the reader can seek solace in the fact that the novel might have an ending just outside his field of vision, that it concludes on the page after the last one she is given. But this offers scant comfort indeed, particularly if one follows the suggestions of inconclusiveness that the last 138 pages offer to its logical conclusion.

The true effect of the last page of this text is not to glide the reader out with a sense of completion as in a myth, a romance, a high mimetic, or many low mimetic works, but—like those of García Márquez, as we shall see next—to cast her back into the book's intricacies, densities, convolutions, incompletions, and uncertainties. For in the world according to Pynchon there exists a beautiful and elusive female center whose name could be Victoria, Vhesissu, Venezuela, Veronica, Valetta, or an infinite number of other possibilities; the exquisite arc of a V-2 screaming down somewhere, sometime, inevitable but unknowable; a universal and rackety Tupperware party where we all stand slightly drunk, slightly hallucinating, and celebrate our ignorance, our absolute inability to know, and our ultimate bewilderment in the face of it all.

# 6

# *Misfires in Eden: García Márquez and Narrative Frustration*

> These are not the times to go around thinking about weddings.
> García Márquez (*One Hundred Years*, 98)

Gabriel García Márquez' projects approach the conventionally improbable and impossible as though they were mimetic, as though they were just "everyday" happenings, so that José Arcadio commits suicide and a trickle of blood from his wounds winds its way across town, down steps and over curbs, around corners and under closed doors, hugging walls so as not to damage the rugs, all the way to Úrsula's feet, as she stands in the kitchen preparing to crack thirty-six eggs to make bread. And his projects approach the conventionally mimetic and "everyday" as though they were sparkling with mystery and magic, to the point where ice is not ice, but the "enormous, transparent block with infinite internal needles in which the light of the sunset was broken up into colored stars" (*One Hundred Years*, 18). That is, García Márquez confounds the marvelous with the mimetic modes of discourse, wrenches conventional perception, and charges his texts with an absurd humor, so that in his universe an angel can plunge out of the sky and thwack face down in the mud, mumbling in what may be Norwegian, toothless, bald, lousy, even unable to get a simple miracle right: blind men grow teeth, a paralytic almost wins a lottery, a leper sprouts sunflowers out of his sores.

The subtexts of these hyperbolic narratives display despair and frustration. Colonel Aureliano Buendía, for instance, leaves off making his little gold fish at ten after four one afternoon because he hears a parade; he walks out of his room and strolls to the street door, mingling with the bystanders that have gathered there. He watches the parade pass, and then "once more he saw the face of the miserable solitude when everything had passed by and there was nothing but the bright expanse of the street and the air full of flying ants with a few onlookers peering into the precipice of uncertainty" (272–73). He wanders over to the chestnut tree and leans against it, and when his family finds him the next morning he is dead.

The colonel searches for distraction from his solitude in a parade of laughter, and at first the universe seems full with events, with things, and with life. But at its center beats an absence registered by the plod of the language—the redundancy of sentence structure, the announcement of void in the string of conjunctions without complexity or vitality—where the very syntax bespeaks a vacuum, a "miserable solitude" that floats back into place just under the frolic. All that remains for the colonel in this passage, which could serve as an emblem for the whole of García Márquez' fictional complex, is a vacant expanse of street, flying ants, uncertainty, and withdrawal. The passage begins with life and ends with death; begins with action and ends with entropy; begins with noise and ends with silence. It announces the inability to create supraworlds, wonderlands, Edens of compensation and redemption that shine forth in the universe of marvelous discourse.

A number of critics have faulted García Márquez for his tendency toward this kind of narrative frustration. Often they have confused narrative failure with failure of narrative. Luis Harss and Barbara Dohmann, for instance, say that the result of the "interwoven plots and subplots, overlappings and backtrackings,

[and] involuted time play" in *Leaf Storm*, comprised of monologues of a woman, her son, and her father attending a wake for a reclusive doctor, "is not density but monotony." And Harss and Dohmann go on to complain that "there are cryptic references, suppressions, blanks, blind spots. We often seem to be on the verge of a revelation that never comes" (323). Even a good deal more rigorous critic like George McMurray finds problems with a story such as "One Day After Saturday"—a tale about how hundreds of birds begin flying through screens in Macando one day—because "the result is . . . an overall impression of needless obscurity" (59). Regina Janes trips up "The Night of the Curlews"—a story about three nameless men blinded by curlews, who sit in a courtyard and talk about nothing special—because it "reverts to deliberate uncertainties" (22).

Once again, then, we come across a cluster of critics who judge one set of conventions by another. What they imply is that all narrative should be limpid, compensatory, certain, complete, easy-to-follow, stable, and simply understood. Their comments also point to the frustration, and hence serve as a springboard for my own discussion of what García Márquez calls the "lost chord" (Harss and Dohmann, 337), in his writing—that nameless thing that drifts up continually, causing the narrative to decenter and jam.

García Márquez was born on March 6, 1928, with an umbilical cord around his neck, in Aracataca, a small town near the Atlantic coast of Colombia. He was the oldest of sixteen children, the son of a telegraph operator and a well-to-do woman whose family opposed the match. His maternal grandparents raised him for his first eight years. His grandfather, whom he has called the most important figure in his life, used to tell him stories about Colombia's civil wars (there were sixty-five to eighty of them between 1820 and 1903) and of nearby towns, one of which was named Macando, a banana plantation whose heyday occurred from 1915 to 1918. His grandmother told him stories of supernatural worlds in a perfectly natural way—of the ghosts who inhabited their house, of an aunt who wove her own funeral shroud, of a neighbor who claimed her daughter had not eloped but ascended to heaven.

When nineteen, García Márquez began studying law at the National University of Colombia in Bogotá, and the same year (1947) he published his first short stories in a local newspaper. A year after that he began a career in journalism, writing film criticism and editorials. In 1955, at twenty-seven, he published his first novel, *Leaf Storm*, and the idea originally surfaced of writing a chronicle about a town named Macando and a colonel named Aureliano Buendía. As a correspondent he traveled widely in Europe, and in 1958 married his Colombian sweetheart. In the early 1960's he settled in Mexico, had two sons, began working as a journalist, public-relations agent, and movie–script writer, while writing a number of novels on the side. In 1982 he won the Nobel Prize for Literature.

García Márquez, like Pynchon, despises ceremony and public speaking, and has said that he became a writer "out of timidity. My real inclination is to be a conjuror, but I get so confused when I try to perform a trick that I've had to take refuge in the solitude of literature." His intelligence is antiabstract and antiacademic. "It's as though," he has said, "they gave the Nobel Prize to a bullfighter" (Guibert, 320 and 336).

In his 1973 study of Latin American literature, D. P. Gallagher comments: "Most contemporary Latin American writing is indeed about failure of some kind or another, failure to materialize a glimpsed idea" (90). He does not go on to explore this idea fully, but it seems another way of saying it is that the primary concern of the Latin American novel is frustration.

To a certain extent, of course, the same could be said about any kind of novel, and narrative, since every narrative to some degree challenges reader-expectations, continually decenters its possibilities, keeps the reader guessing, and keeps on thwarting those guesses. That is how a text generates narrative tension and interest. Only the least complex narrative forms deliver exactly what they say they will deliver. Most narratives employ conventions to subvert them in some way or another. For many, the narrative that lacks all frustration—the Harlequin Romance, for instance—lacks all interest. In this way, Gallagher's statement is accurate but obvious.

But there is a second way to take his claim. When he mentions contemporary Latin American writing, he has in mind the fictions of Borges, Vargas Llosa, García Márquez and Cabrera Infante—four postmodern fantasts by my definition. Seen in this light, Gallagher's comment becomes more interesting, for while almost any narrative carries with it a charge of frustration on some stratum, postmodern fantasy carries with it a terrific charge of frustration on every stratum. In the fantastic mode, and particularly the mode as it functions in postmodern texts, anything can happen. And if that is the case, then everything can happen. And consequently every sentence contains so many possibilities that the reader's expectations are necessarily blocked. Hence, the fantastic text forces her to float in a freeplay of potentialities, unable to imagine a consistent narrative future.

Frustration arises for a number of reasons. It results from an inability to bounce back after a number of setbacks in narrative expectations, from a sense that one can no longer master one's fictional environment, no longer clearly decode the system of conventions the writer is employing. It results from the disjunction between the narrative goal the reader imagines and the narrative goal the text produces. And the intensity of that frustration is a function of how much the reader wants the goal he has imagined, to what extent the narrative delegitimizes the goal, and how many times the reader's imagination has been devalued by the textual imagination. It results at moments when the reader experiences unrelieved defeat, the inability to believe he can do anything to improve incomprehensible conditions, the inability to imagine a compensatory and stable narrative future.

Consequently, the reader finds herself befuddled before a narrative like *The Unnamable* or *Gravity's Rainbow*. But compared to these difficult texts, the projects of García Márquez at first glance seem exceptions to the rule—particularly with a work like *One Hundred Years of Solitude*. Yet on closer examination, one finds this is not the case. Alongside apparently "easy" texts like *One Hundred Years*, García Márquez has also produced such "hard" ones as *Leaf Storm*, *The Autumn of the Patriarch*, and "Nabo" (1951), the last of which is a Faulknerian tale that employs temporal involutions and unstable points-of-view to explore the relationship between a delirious man and a mute girl. And even *One Hundred Years*, as we shall see, breeds frustration at various textual strata.

My students delight in García Márquez' imagination, in the wild events he conjures, in his dazzling disruption of logic, and in his hilariously playful plots. They delight, that is, until pressed for specifics, for exactly what has happened and when and to whom. Then the idea of narrative frustration surfaces, discomfort announces itself, and it soon becomes apparent that García Márquez' projects dismantle Balzacian conventions concerning storytelling. His plots may appear linear—after all, *One Hundred Years* has a beginning, middle, and end, and *The Autumn of the Patriarch* clearly describes the youth, rise to power, middle-age, slip in power, and old age of a Caribbean dictator—but on closer inspection they reveal themselves as spirals of digressions, digressions within digressions, clarifications and reclarifications to the point where nothing is clear, data upon data until one can hardly remember a thing.

*One Hundred Years*, for instance, begins with the now-famous line: "Many years later, as he faced the firing squad, Colonel Aureliano Buendía was to remember that distant afternoon when his father took him to discover ice." And so, it would appear, a narrative has begun. A tale is being told. What a reader used to the Balzacian mode should expect is a recounting of that distant afternoon, a description of the father perhaps, a memory about the discovery of ice. Or perhaps already she is slightly shaken, placed slightly off balance, as she senses the sentence's dislocation of time in the phrase "many years later" (many years later than what? when is all this happening?), or the destabilization of the mimetic in the last words of the sentence (the discovery of *ice*? since when is ice treated as a scientific discovery?).

With the second sentence ("At that time"—again, when?—"Macando was a village of twenty adobe houses . . . ") the spiral begins turning, and the narrative digresses into the first days of Macando; into the arrival of the gypsies in March; into a description of Melquíades, José Arcadio Buendía, Úrsula Iguarán; into an account of José Arcadio's romp with magnets, telescopes, and magnifying glasses, and his eventual setting out along the northern route into the jungles; and into the discovery (and the center of the first chapter are the ideas of discovery and unveiling) of the galleon. This continues for fifteen pages, until the digressions within digressions finally end for a brief moment, and the initial narrative resurfaces: "Those hallucinating sessions remained printed on the memories of the boys in such a way that many years later, a second before the regular army officer gave the firing squad the command to fire . . . " (16). Then, for two short pages, the discovery of ice is recounted. Afterwards, it sinks back into the text, not to rise again for another sixty-five pages (83). In other fictions, such as "Nabo," *Leaf Storm*, or *The Autumn of the Patriarch* (which García Márquez calls "really an extremely long poem" [Guibert, 328]), he abandons any sense of conventional plot altogether, and forces narrative from a horizontal to a vertical plane, thereby creating a lyrical parody of the Balzacian mode.

A much less obvious way by which García Márquez generates narrative frustration is his frequent use of doubles. This device signals a literal split in personality, psychological misdevelopment, self-fragmentation, and the blurring and decomposition of the ego; a dislocation in personhood that is antithetical to conventional notions of character. In *Leaf Storm*, for instance, when the priest walks into the room where the old doctor who will soon hang himself is lying, he notices "the extraordinary resemblance between the two men. They weren't exact, but they looked like brothers. . . . there was a community of features between them that exists between two brothers" (121). In the story "Blacaman the Good, Vendor of Miracles" (1968), about a picaro who recounts his bizarre adventures with his cruel charlatan of a boss, Blacaman the Good and Blacaman the Bad are mirror images of each other. An earlier tale, "The Other Side of Death" (1948), in which a dead man describes his old body, a linguistic split in pronouns between "he" and "I" signals a doubling of personality, a questioning of subject-object relations. In *One Hundred Years*, sets of characters represent the matter and antimatter of being: the José Arcadios are impulsive, enterprising, and often scientists, while the Aurelianos are lucid, withdrawn, and often poets. Melquíades is the perfect writer, while Aureliano the perfect reader. Úrsula holds the Latin American house of Atreus together, while Amaranta finally destroys it. Patricio Aragonés doubles the despot in *The Autumn of the Patriarch*, and the despot's sadistic right-hand man, José Ignacio Saenz de la Barra, creates "a secret empire within his own private empire, an invisible service of repression and extermination" (195), a double of the original one. The dictator himself recognizes the "very ancient certainty that the most feared enemy is within oneself in the confidence of the heart" (109)—that the other is the dark double of the self.

Doubling questions ontology and epistemology. It produces textual schizophrenia. This frustration of the Balzacian character arises appropriately in *Leaf Storm*, where there is a gap reminiscent of Sutpen's in *Absalom, Absalom!*:

> I've never been able to find out whether his papers were really in order or not. I couldn't find out if he was French, as we supposed, or if he had any remembrance of a family, which he must have had but about which he never said a word. . . . That day—after five years of living in the same house—I suddenly realized that we didn't even know his name (78).

Early in *The Autumn of the Patriarch*, the townspeople enter the presidential palace and find the body of the solitary despot:

"Only when we turned him over to look at his face did we realize that it was impossible to recognize him, even though his face had not been pecked away by vultures, because none of us had ever seen him" (10).

A passage that could serve as an emblem of the problem appears in *One Hundred Years*, when the narrator discusses the characters of José Arcadio Segundo and Aureliano Segundo:

> They were so much alike and so mischievous during childhood that not even Santa Sofía de la Piedad could tell them apart. On the day of the christening Amaranta put bracelets on them with their respective names and dressed them in different colored clothing marked with each one's initials, but when they began to go to school they decided to exchange clothing and bracelets and call each other by opposite names. The teacher, Melchor Excalona, used to knowing José Arcadio Segundo by his green shirt, went out of his mind when he discovered that the latter was wearing Aureliano Segundo's bracelet. . . . From then on he was never sure who was who. Even when they grew up and life made them different, Úrsula still wondered if they themselves might not have made a mistake in some moment of their intricate game of confusion and had become changed forever (187).

This registers the relationship between reader and character in the text. Here, Santa Sofía de la Piedad, Melchor Excalona, and Úrsula function as befuddled students of literature, struggling to find out some core identity, "never sure who [is] who," blocked at every moment by the characters themselves. Because of the elfish repetition of names in the text, the book is accompanied by a diagram carefully plotting out the family line. What soon becomes apparent is that the diagram hinders far more than it helps. It announces the complexity and inevitable frustration of the book. It transforms text into test, reading into a problematics of mnemonics, and love of the text into desire.

Character becomes opaque, and human actions become incomprehensible.

In his *Labyrinth of Solitude*—a phrase that could serve as an alternate title to many of García Márquez' works—Octavio Paz argues that "self-discovery is above all the realization that we are alone: it is the opening of an impalpable, transparent wall—that of our consciousness—between the world and ourselves" (9). More, "man is nostalgia and a search for communion. Therefore, when he is aware of himself he is aware of his lack of another, that is, of his solitude" (195). This poetics of isolation throbs at the center of all that García Márquez has produced. "It's the only subject I've written about" (Guibert, 314), he says. His texts are writings of radical separation.

Monologic structures, indications of this labyrinth of solitude, abound in García Márquez' work. In his first novel, three consciousnesses are isolated from each other and from the rest of the community in a hot, oppressive, bad-smelling room, the center of which is filled by a coffin (a register of the absence at the center of the text, a reminder of the final and complete isolation of death) of the doctor who has committed suicide after living alone in the house for years. In "A Very Old Man with Enormous Wings" (1968), the tale of the angel who falls from the sky, the protagonist is locked away in a chicken coop in the same way Kafka's Hunger Artist is locked away in his cage. The couple keeping him there, Pelayo and Elisenda, come out of their house one morning to find "the whole neighborhood in front of the chicken coop having fun with the angel, without the slightest reverence, tossing him things to eat through the openings in the wire as if he weren't a supernatural creature but a circus animal" (*Leaf Storm*, 159). The angel is not only isolated physically from the community, but also linguistically. He is shut off in a "hermetic language" (*Leaf Storm*, 162), and sometimes falls delirious "with the tongue twisters of an old Norwegian" (*Leaf Storm*, 166). "The Last Voyage of the Ghost Ship" (1968) consists of one sentence that stretches for eight pages, a monologue by a boy whose tone oscillates between self-assertion and self-repudiation as he dreams of a large ocean liner which continually veers toward invisible shoals, runs aground, and sinks. García Márquez carries the same linguistic structure into *The Autumn of the Patriarch*, a structure that echoes the life of "the most solitary man on earth" (30). The whole of the text is a kind of running monologue, or system of intersecting monologues by voices unaware of each other. It is divided into six circular configurations, each of which begins with the dictator's death, then digresses, and finally ends up with a major event in his life.

Very few characters actually speak to each other in García Márquez' narratives. Little dialogue—the sign of communication and communion—occurs. No one breaks through his Samsa-like "hard shell of . . . solitude" (*One Hundred Years*, 174). In fact, often no one speaks but the narrator, who does so from the seemingly omniscient point-of-view of God. But this deity-narrator is an absurd divinity, like that angel who falls from the sky, since all he really knows about are actions, not thoughts. Nor is he omnipotent. All he can do is stand back and watch the world decompose, unable to reverse the entropic movement of the cosmos, and unable to free himself from his own isolation.

Perhaps the most well-known monologic structure in García Márquez' output is the image of incest in *One Hundred Years*. It is an image of solitude, of exclusion from community, of the impossibility of diversity and change, of autistic single-mindedness, of the limited capacity for love and the infinite capacity for desire, of egocentricity, of introspection decayed into a disease of consciousness. Paz writes:

> In archaic societies, a complex and rigid system of prohibitions, rules and rituals protects the individual from solitude. The group is the only source of health. The solitary man is the invalid, a dead branch that must be lopped off and burned, for society as a whole is endangered if one of its components becomes ill (205).

Consequently, societies place rigid restrictions on incest and extreme solitude. In Macando, the original sin appears in the form of a boy with a pig's tail born to Úrsula's aunt and José Arcadio Buendía's uncle. For seven generations the family lives in terror of a recurrence of the pig's tail, a recurrence that inevitably occurs when the last of the Buendías—Aureliano Babilonia and his aunt Amaranta Úrsula—perform incest.

The result of incest, the pig's tail, has a number of psychological implications. Bettelheim tells the story of "Hans, My Hedgehog," wherein a man frustrated by his wife's inability to produce children comments one day: "I want a child, even if it should be a hedgehog." Soon thereafter his wish is granted—in full. His wife gives birth to a child whose upper torso is that of a hedgehog, and whose lower is that of a boy. Bettelheim goes on to interpret: "The psychological wisdom of these tales is remarkable: lack of control over emotions on the part of the parent creates a child who is a misfit. In fairy tales and dream, physical malformation often stands for psychological misdevelopment" (70). And physical malformation is everywhere in García Márquez' texts: women turned into spiders or cats, men who become snakes or jelly or suddenly blossom the wings of bats. Such miscreations point to emotional malfunctioning, perverted desire, and frustrated procreation.

Another source of misfires has to do with the notion of time in García Márquez' projects. In the Balzacian mode, time is chronology, sequence, order, progression, unfolding, revealing, continuity, and a change of state. In the projects of García Márquez, on the other hand, time is stalled, decreated, made to repeat itself again and again, the highlight of a failed hope for past or future. Among the moderns such as Yeats, Proust, or Eliot, the artist through art can transcend time into a beatific realm of timeless perfection. Among the postmoderns such as Kafka, Beckett, or Pynchon, time goes nowhere but in circles, or does nothing but run down. Transcendence becomes unimaginable. In the texts of García Márquez, postmodern time has affinities with that of Nietzsche. For him, if the universe is finite and the structure of matter discrete, then there are only a finite number of possible successive configurations to the universe. Given enough time, then, all the atoms of the universe will eventually return to the configuration they had at a previous time, and the universe will live again exactly as it had before. For García Márquez, of course, the situation is not so technical. Perhaps the universe will not repeat itself again and again exactly the way it has done before, but the same patterns will emerge, the same hoped-for futures and the same failed futures, the same kinds of characters and the same kinds of frustrations.

In his projects, there exist cyclical recurrences, archetypal patterns, Borgesian structures that give the lie to compensatory time and to hope for learning from the past. "The notion of time" in his work "disappeared completely" (*Leaf Storm*, 205). The mayor in *In Evil Hour* is struck by "the impression that time had stopped" (142), and at the end of that text the reader realizes she is really back to where she began. Úrsula "confirmed her impression that time was going in a circle" (226). In *The Autumn of the Patriarch* a pattern of infinite circularity emerges. A continual swinging back to the death of the despot takes place so that there is never a sense of forward progress. The same holds true with *Chronicle of a Death Foretold*, the story of an innocent dandy who is murdered for deflowering a macho's bride and of the town who allows the murder to happen, where the narrative continually circles back to the moment of the death, a few minutes one morning.

Narrative frustration also arises from the reader's inability to know, to locate the center of meaning in a text, or to perceive the textual universe clearly. Even in terms of categorizing a given text, of plugging it into a larger grid, it is difficult to stabilize García Márquez' projects. While one can talk about affinities between Kafka's work and Expressionism, Borges' and Conceptual Art, Robbe-Grillet's and New Realism, Beckett's and Minimalism, Fuentes' and Op Art, Pynchon's and Pop Art, the very act of categorization of text like *One Hundred Years* causes frustration. It continually floats and remains unfastened.

García Márquez' works register this sense of uncertainty in another way as well. In his universe, man is scientist, a detective of ontology, who, like José Arcadio with his magnets, ice, sextant, and so forth, searches for understanding. Yet he is forever thwarted by its absence. *In Evil Hour*, for instance, is a detective story about an unnamed town in the midst of The Violence, a brutal civil war between conservatives and liberals in Colombia that lasted from the late forties into the sixties, causing the death of several hundred thousand people, where suddenly one day anonymous notes revealing personal secrets and accusing various townspeople of wrongdoing appear tacked on doors and walls. The characters search for some sort of clue that will point to the perpetrator or perpetrators who are originating this "terrorism in the moral order" (115). In pursuit of answers, the town mayor goes to a fortune teller, Casandra—whose predictions in Greek myth were never believed—to ask her who the culprit or culprits are. After studying her cards for quite a while, she announces her conclusion: "It's the whole town and it's nobody" (133). The Other is everywhere. Even though the guards walk the streets at night, and a host of people are questioned, the town slips into mass paranoia, and the mystery is never solved. A scapegoat is finally killed, but the reader is not sure whether that has in fact changed anything or not.

"An atmosphere of uncertainty" (41)—and the word "uncertainty" appears often in the text—pervades *One Hundred Years*. Characters are difficult to tell apart, the geography remains vague, the time frame is confused. In *Autumn of the Patriarch* indeterminacy even slips into the linguistic level of the book. A "tremor of uncertainty" (105) flickers in the language. Every sentence is unsure of itself, entropic, apocalyptic, its syntax collapsing and drifting toward the void. Every sentence is jammed with catalogs, sense impressions, plot details, to the point where it becomes unwieldy, tumbling in on itself, becoming a parody of

Balzacian faith in language, always announcing, like the despot's government, that "there was always another truth behind the truth" (45). And the same notion of a decentered truth arises in *Chronicle*, where the townspeople cannot even be sure of the weather ("Many people coincided in recalling that it was a radiant morning with a sea breeze coming in through the banana groves. . . . But most agreed that the weather was funereal, with a cloudy, low sky and the thick smell of still waters" [4]), let alone who deflowered Angela:

> she would recount [the story] in all its details to anyone who wanted to hear it, except for one item that would never be cleared up: who was the real cause of her damage, and how and why, because no one believed that it had really been Santiago Nasar (89).

Last, I should like to approach narrative frustration in García Márquez' projects from the angle of endings: the emblem of closure, completion, wholeness, symmetry, conclusion, final understanding, harmony, and order. Every piece of art must end in some way. Music finishes—Cage's begins—in silence. Every painting ends in the frame or the blankness that comes after it. Every piece of writing ends in the lack that appears after the covers are closed. Ending in the Balzacian and marvelous modes is an impulse toward enclosure, pattern, and fulfillment. As Frank Kermode suggests, there exists a deep need in bourgeois consciousness to believe it belongs to things around it, that it is related to a "world" that forms a narrative with a beginning and end. It needs to believe in an aesthetic of an end, The End, the ultimate gathering together, and hence throughout history it has been marking off Ends (chapter one).

Postmodern fantasy, however, resists the idea of closure and wholeness. It subverts the notion of endings, casts it into a state of peripeteia, denies its redemption. Although their texts must physically end, postmodern fantasts strive against conclusion. Kafka will not finish his larger projects. Robbe-Grillet's fantasies spin around and around, repeating themselves forever. Beckett's run down, move toward entropy, but will not conclude. Pynchon's promise closure but deliver deferredness.

García Márquez works against Balzacian closure in another way. His texts, as Allen Thiher argues, are

> the defeat of the Hegelian logos, the fall of logos, with an unsurpassed rage. The fall into silence at the end of [*One Hundred Years*], the coming of exile from the memory of men, is an anti-eschatology that undoes Western historiography from its biblical sources through Marx. . . . there is no sign of redemption. History is reduced to the paradoxical record of its own fall (207).

*The Autumn of the Patriarch* and *Chronicle* end so many times that finally the idea is placed in brackets. Always his texts end in some sort of failure—in storms, decompositions, in running downs—that serves as an emblem for the failure of the text to attain compensation and progress. The result is what Thiher calls "texticide"—a notion that "is at one with the anti-theological gestures that characterize postmodern thought and fiction" (209). The transcendental signified is decomposed. Consequently, *Leaf Storm* ends in stasis, with an eleven-year-old boy following a coffin out of a house, thinking about curlews, waiting for something to happen. *In Evil Hour* ends with a malicious government taking the place of a malicious government, as the mayor has a young man tortured to death, hence launching an authoritarian regime. *The Autumn of the Patriarch* ends with the despot in a state of entropy, where nothing has been learned, nothing has been fulfilled, nothing has been made whole except for absence—that which lies at the core of J. M. Coetzee's project.

# ❦ 7 ❦

# *The Presence of Absence:*
# *Coetzee's* Waiting for the Barbarians

> There is only a blankness, and desolation that there has to be such blankness.
> Coetzee (*Waiting for the Barbarians*, 73)

John M. Coetzee was born in Cape Town, South Africa, in 1940. He grew up in the midst of an unwieldy and corrupt system of apartheid—a system capable of destroying opposition before it has had a chance to get its message out, before it can articulate its cause. Coetzee attended school in South Africa and America, studying computer science and linguistics, then returned to teach at the University of Cape Town, lecturing on linguistics, American and English literature, and producing criticism on, among others, Defoe, Gibbon, Swift, and Kafka. He has often acknowledged the presence in his projects of Kafka's absurdity, unintelligibility before the Law, paranoia, and textual terrorism; Faulkner's concern with isolation, decadence, and the language of consciousness; Beckett's sense of being-there and his existential horror; and Robbe-Grillet's attempt at primary language, a style of absence.

When thirty-four, Coetzee published his first novel, *Dusklands* (1974), the double-tale of Eugene Dawn who, in the process of making out a report on the propaganda techniques used in Vietnam for the U.S. government, slowly loses his mind; and Jacobus Coetzee, a Christian who in precolonial times pushes deep into the heart of Africa, into the land of the Namaqua Hottentots, who brutalize and degrade him and send him back to civilization where he organizes a small army and returns on a punitive raid. Three years later, Coetzee published *In the Heart of the Country* (1977), a novel that comes in the form of some unidentifiable kind of writing, perhaps a diary, of a young woman who is isolated with her father and several servants on a farm in a no-man's land. Three years after that Coetzee published *Waiting for the Barbarians* (1980), which, after being held under embargo by the South African government for several months before being released in Coetzee's country, won the James Tait Black Memorial Prize, the Geoffry Faber Award, and the South African CNA Literary Prize.

The novel opens on a frontier settlement, where a rumor is circulating that the barbarians in the hills are regrouping in preparation for a massive invasion. The desert settlement, the first line of defense for the Empire, is placed on alert and its magistrate is brought out of his complacency when Colonel Joll, representative from the Empire, appears with two barbarian prisoners, a father and son, whom Joll tortures until told what he wants to hear. Then he sets out for more prisoners, and soon returns with a host of them, whom he tortures and places in a makeshift jail until they end up making such a mess that they are set free. The magistrate comes upon a barbarian girl who is left behind. Joll has gotten to her too: she has been partially blinded and her feet have been broken. The magistrate takes her in and makes her a scullery maid, oscillating between desiring her and feeling indifferent to her presence. After several months, he decides to take her back to her people, and, with a handful of men, sets out on a brutal three-week journey across marshland and desert. A small group of barbarians play cat-and-mouse with the men until they pause just long enough to meet and take the girl back. When the magistrate returns to the settlement, he is arrested by Joll for consorting with the enemy, jailed, and humiliated until he is broken, at which point he is set free. Rumors of the ever-present barbarian invasion mount, people begin abandoning the settlement in convoys, and soldiers are withdrawn in large numbers. The magistrate returns to his old apartment and, while waiting for the barbarian attack, sets about writing a record of his last year.

Whereas some works of art, Coetzee has said, "reinforce the myths of our culture, others dissect these myths. In our time and place, it is the latter kind of work that seems to me more urgent" (Wood, 14). His is a writing that recharts, interrogates, challenges, and dismantles dominant cultural myths like "civilization," "humanism," and "authority" by revealing their opposite. On the other side of these myths of presence lies the realization of the woman who narrates Coetzee's second novel: "instead of being a womanly warmth at the heart of this house I have been a zero, a null, a vacuum towards which all collapses inward" (2).

Perhaps for this reason, early reviews of *Waiting for the Barbarians* were not as postive as one might expect, given the number of literary awards it received. Several reviews, like that by Jean Marquard, faulted the book on ethical grounds. He trips up South African novels in general because "the effectiveness . . . depends on the measure of disgust they can arouse in the reader," the action occurring "inside the mind of a character from whom the reader is alienated" (*Contrast*, 45). Others, like Leon Whiteson, fault it on aesthetic grounds:

> The geography is garbled: there is desert and snow, lizards and bears. The story is told in that most awkward tense: the historic present. The dialogue is stiff, the writing has the air of a translation. . . . Coetzee's bad dreams have not been earned by any truth. . . . The heart of this novel is not darkness but mush (26).

Irving Howe, in his generally favorable review that appeared on the front page of the *New York Times Book Review*, argues that "one possible loss is bite and pain, the urgency that a specified historical place and time may provide." These are nostalgic readings. Under the rhetoric, Marquard believes novels should be compensatory; Whiteson believes they should be Balzacian in setting, logic, tense, and style; and Howe believes they should be mimetic.

But a number of reviews attempted understanding rather than prescribing. Howe himself, for instance, elsewhere in his discussion of the book argues that it is a political tale about South Africa. "Mr. Coetzee," he writes, "tells the story of an imaginary Empire, set in an unspecified place and time, yet recognizable as a 'universalized' version of South Africa. . . . The result is a realistic fable." The heart of the text for Howe is a "clash of moral styles, a drama of representative ways of governing"—a field of tension among the magistrate's faded humanism, Joll's neofascism, and barbarian anarchy.

George Steiner reads the book as a Hegelian parable about the interdependence of the master and the slave. For Hegel, those who risk least in the struggle for power become the slaves of those who risk the most. The slave submits to the master who uses him as a means to his own ends. The master's consumption depends on the slave's work and the slave's work depends upon the master's consumption and will to power. In Coetzee's text, the Empire cannot exist without the presence of its opposite, and Joll cannot exist without the presence of the magistrate. As we have seen with Kafka (K. and the Law), Borges (the dreamer and the dreamed), Robbe-Grillet (the jealous husband-lover and A . . . ), Beckett (the narrator of *How It Is* and Pim), Fuentes (Aura and Felipe), Pynchon (Oedipa and Tristero) and García Márquez (the patriarch and his countrymen), we all need our scapegoats, and our scapegoats need us.

I should like to emphasize the absence at the center of fantasy's language, the gaps at the center of its projects, the revelations of nothing that make themselves felt throughout Coetzee's third novel. This concern, as well as the other related ones I shall deal with in this chapter, brings my essay full circle, from the omega back to the alpha, from a great-grandson back to the primogenitor of contemporary fantasy: Kafka.

His name has drifted to the surface in each chapter as an emblem of autism, language-in-crisis, unstable metamorphosis, ontological and epistemological uncertainty, unfulfilled desire, postcultural anarchy, postmodern madness and despair, anti-logic, failed gaming, acidic irony, dehumanization, the literary equivalent of silence, the contemporary detective, and the blaster of space and time. Using Borges' comment in his essay "Kafka and His Precursors"—that "the fact is that every writer *creates* his own precursors. His work modifies our conception of the past, as it will modify the future" (*Labyrinths*, 201)—as a springboard, Allen Thiher notes:

> We read Kafka through the lens of intertextuality, in the sense that our contemporary fictions have taught us to read what Kafka's immediate contemporaries could not see. To reverse what Borges said about Kafka . . . we must read in turn most of our contemporary writers by making of the Czech writer their precursor, perhaps the most important precursor for what many now call postmodern fiction ("Kafka's Legacy," 543).

Just at the moment of modernism's apex, when Joyce and Proust and Rilke and the rest were achieving their most famous texts, Kafka entered and ruptured modernism's security and sense of power by generating a mode of discourse that "puts constantly into question its own quest for representation, revelation, and meaning" (546).

Coetzee's debt to Kafka in *Waiting for the Barbarians* is clear. While there are many, perhaps the strongest Kafkaesque echo comes from "An Old Manuscript," which begins: "It looks as if much had been neglected in our country's system of defense. We have not concerned ourselves with it until now and have gone about our daily work; but things that have been happening recently begin to trouble us" (*The Penal Colony*, 145–47). The "manuscript" is by a cobbler whose workshop sits across from the Emperor's palace. One day the cobbler realizes the barbarians from the north have infiltrated the town. No one seems to notice them as they busy themselves sharpening swords, whittling arrows, and practicing horsemanship. They are filthy, and communication with them is impossible: "They do not know our language, indeed they hardly have a language of their own. . . . Our way of living and our institutions they neither understand nor care to understand" (146). Even their horses are carnivorous and malicious; and at one point the barbarians themselves devour a live ox. The "manuscript" concludes with the narrator asking: "What is going to happen?" The guards have abandoned their posts. No one knows how long it will be before the barbarians turn on the townspeople. And, somehow, all this "is a misunderstanding of some kind; and it will be the ruin of us" (147).

Like Coetzee's text, Kafka's takes the form of an old manuscript written by a man knowing the end is near, that a new barbarian age is upon the town, that all that is left is waiting. Both texts are fragments, remainders of a lost age, manuscripts of despair and frustration. The center of both Coetzee's and Kafka's universes is the Emperor's palace. This is implied in Coetzee's text, made explicit in Kafka's. But in both cases the palace is a lack, a hidden center. The Emperor, like meaning, has withdrawn to the innermost garden, or stands watching from a window, removed. Both are stories of slow terrorism, about neglecting a country's system of defense, about the failure to break through a sense of everydayness until it is too late, about the slow giving oneself over to the Other, the manifestation of entropy, the breakdown of the old beliefs of civilization and the rise of dehumanism, and about dying races. Both texts end in hesitation, uncertainty, just at the edge of postcultural anarchy. Kafka's concludes wondering what will happen next, and realizing that all has been a communication fizzle, something beyond comprehension. And the same could be said about Coetzee's. At the heart of each stands the barbarian, a void that has no language of its own, that neither understands nor cares to understand.

Another notion the texts share is that of waiting, an idea that appears frequently in postmodern fantasy. Elsewhere, K. waits for the Law to judge him. Borges' narrator in "Tlön, Uqbar, Orbis Tertius" waits for the invasion of reality by dream. Didi and Gogo wait for Godot. García Márquez' cantankerous colonel walks down to the mailboat every Friday to wait for his pension that never arrives. Such waiting points to the lack of something that will not show itself, the inability to know fully, and impossibility.

Most of all, waiting points to what is not there—absence. Clearly all texts present absences at their core in one way or another, but not all believe they do. With respect to this, Jacques Derrida discusses what he calls a metaphysics of presence, a metaphysics that longs for the truth behind every sign, the belief that the reader of a text can pass from signifier to the signified which is a stable meaning. In the model of presence, writing is a process whereby an author sends his message to the world and the reader retrieves that message and tries to find out what the writer had in mind. But however appropriate this model may appear with regard to speech, Derrida argues, such a model with respect to the written word is at best the confession of a yearning for an edenic world where no system of mediation called language or writing exists between form and meaning. But the very act of writing severs the word from the writers, and without the presence of the writer, the word's "meaning" and "truth" become absent. Hence, to write is to produce gaps that must be supplemented, to produce signs which provoke the reader to a kind of rewriting. To this extent, writing is cut off from any absolute responsibility, from any ultimate authority. It becomes orphaned from its father, open to alternate parents. It becomes an absence which must be filled.

Texts of mimetic discourse believe that the word represents the world, that writing re-presents "reality." But texts of fantastic discourse not only believe in the absent center; they revel in its possibilities and drift in the freeplay of its potential. In the postlapsarian universe of postmodern fantasy, there lives only a schism between word and world.

Even the title of Coetzee's text points to this absence—and words like "blank," "blind," "space," and "empty" appear frequently throughout the text. And absence announces the presence of a detective story. The reader, the magistrate, and others try to piece together clues about who the barbarians are, what they are like, and what they want. But, as we have often seen, the end never comes. The nomads never overrun the settlement. "Meaning" once again is deferred. By the end, the magistrate feels "like a man who lost his way long ago but presses on along a road that may lead nowhere" (156). "To the last," he says, "we will have learned nothing" (143). The people in the settlement have learned nothing about humanity, about civilization, or about themselves. And both the people in the settlement and the reader have learned nothing about the barbarians. And everyone has learned about Nothing, about how absence unfolds.

By pointing to the lack of "a specified historical place and time" and to the fact that "the geography is garbled," Howe and Whiteson indicate other absences in the text—those of clear topography. On first reading, the text may appear more mimetic than many of those I have discussed earlier, but on closer inspection strangeness concerning time and space intrude. When could we be, and where, for instance, that would help us account for the fact that the magistrate does not know what sunglasses are? How can there be snow in a desert? Where do the bearskins that the people wear come from, since there are no bears in the desert? How can there be both sunglasses and the lack of advanced military weapons or motors? Perhaps the geography of this entropic settlement signals the hypnagogic state, but it could also signal the postnuclear terrain of science fiction—the terrain of civilization after The End, as in Beckett's *Endgame* or *All Strange Away*—where sunglasses are throwbacks to an earlier age; where no bodies are found in the ruins;

where the unlucky, the barbarians, wander aimlessly. Here we are in a "haze of desert" (14) where "time has broken" (43), in a "dead country" (98) where there is only a "dead season" (49), in a nightmarish universe where "dust rather than air becomes the medium in which we live. We swim through dust like fish through water" (6).

Each of the characters in this universe is a kind of reader, decoder, and interpreter. The magistrate is not just a "country magistrate . . . serving out [his] days on this lazy frontier," who has "not asked for more than a quiet life in quiet times" (8). He is also an archeologist, an anthropologist, a digger for "meaning," searching those ruins that lie under the dunes around the settlement—ruins that date back before the western provinces were annexed, before the settlement was founded, before, perhaps, even the barbarians. Below the floors there are buried bags that contain wood slips, on which are painted unintelligible characters that are almost illegible because of the sand's action across them. Hoping to decipher this failed language, the magistrate collects all the slips he can, two hundred and fifty-six of them, and wonders:

> Is it by chance that the number is perfect?. . . . I cleared the floor of my office and laid them out, first in one great square, then in sixteen smaller squares, then in other combinations, thinking that what I had hitherto taken to be characters in a syllabary might in fact be elements of a picture whose outline would leap at me if I struck on the right arrangement (16).

In his attempt to decipher them, he finds himself "reading the slips in a mirror, or tracing one on top of another, or conflating half of one with half of another" (16).

In other words, the magistrate is a decoder. "I search for secrets and answers, no matter how bizarre," he writes, "like an old woman reading tea leaves" (44). But in the end he realizes that his slips do not hold a single meaning. It is impossible to tell just what the author(s) had in mind. Rather, he discovers that the slips

> can be read in many orders. Further, each single slip can be read in many ways. Together they can be read as a domestic journal, or they can be read as a plan of war, or they can be turned on their sides and read as a history of the last years of the Empire.

He concludes that "there is no agreement among the scholars about how to interpret these relics" (112). Here is a new version of Kafka's parable "Before the Law," a parable that exhibits only the commentators' despair before the multiplicity of meaning. As Derrida would have it, the wood slips form an absence which may be supplemented in an endless number of ways, nothing more than a productive mechanism.

Joll, on the other hand, is a misreader, a false reader, a believer in the metaphysics of presence: "in his quest for truth he is tireless" (22), says the magistrate. And this is just Joll's problem. He still cryptofascistically reads for "truth," for "answer." He still believes in interpretation and the absolute. For him, behind every signifier there is one and only one signified, so when he comes across the magistrate's slips his response is immediate, and incorrect: "A reasonable inference is that the wooden slips contain messages passed between yourself and other parties, we do not know when. It remains for you to explain what the messages say and who the other parties are" (110). He tries to fix the language of the slips, to decode into compensation. He will kill for the "truth"—and in fact has done so with the barbarian son and father he captured. But the magistrate thinks to himself: "I do not even know whether to read from right to left or from left to right. . . . I have no idea what they stand for" (110). The magistrate believes in the metaphysics of absence, in the idea that "meaning" and "truth" must be allowed to float free, even at the risk of casting the commentators into despair. While Joll believes that there is no system of mediation called language (and hence becomes a proponent of the mimetic mode of discourse), the magistrate believes in decentering "truth" (and hence becomes a proponent of fantastic discourse).

Not only on the stratum of character does absence pervade the text. Images suggesting blankness abound in *Waiting for the Barbarians*. Joll's "two little discs of glass suspended in front of his eyes in loops of wire," for instance, imply his absence of humanism, his spiritual blindness, the lack behind the "mystery of dark shields hiding healthy eyes" (4). Eyes, particularly disfigured eyes, permeate the novel. Not only are there Joll's "blind" (1) eyes, but also those of the boy whose father Joll murders—his "face is puffy and bruised, one eye is swollen shut" (3). The magistrate notices in the corner of the barbarian girl's eye "a greyish puckering as though a caterpillar lay there with its head under the eyelid, grazing" (31). After his beatings by Joll's men, even the magistrate, who cannot *see* what sense the wood slips make, finds that his "left eye is a mere slit" (115). All these images of eyes indicate partial sight, partial blindness, distorted vision, and the fact that in every act of perception exists a gap that cannot be filled. So that even if the reader may feel the need to identify with a moral center in the text—with the magistrate, for instance—such images emphasize the impossibility of such an act.

In addition to images of eyes that signal absence, there appears the image of the magistrate's quest into those buried ruins, where he locates Nothing: "There are no human remains among the ruins. If there is a cemetery we have not found it. The houses contain no furniture" (15). All the barbarian girl can see with her almost blind eye is a lack: "Am I to believe that gazing back at me she sees nothing—my feet perhaps, parts of the room, a hazy circle of light, but at the centre, where I am, only a blur, a blank?" (31), the magistrate asks. The face of the prostitute the magistrate sometimes visits also turns into void: "It occurs to me that I cannot even recall the other one's face. . . . Blank, like a fist beneath a black wig, the face grows out of the throat and out of the blank body beneath it, without aperture, without entry" (42). Even the face that appears again and again in the magistrate's recurring dream reveals Nothing: "The face I see is blank, featureless; it is the face of an embryo or a tiny whale; it is not a face at all but another part of the body that bulges under the skin; it is white; it is the snow itself" (37). It is that which accommodates different readings, that which may be supplemented almost infinitely. The archeologist digs to the center only to find he has been reading through to a void.

Whiteson's comment releases another approach to my discussion of the presence of absence: "The story is told in that most awkward tense: the historic present," he writes. "The dialogue is stiff, the writing has the air of a translation" (8). He comes to the brink of insight only to slip back into prescription. Coetzee's use of the present tense may be seen as a mockery of presence. It is a tense that registers the absence of past and future, and, by drawing attention to itself, forces awareness that it is a fictional tense, that it serves to represent what is not there. In other words, it announces what the magistrate already knows, that "whatever can be articulated is falsely put" (64). To write is to acknowledge a metaphysics of absence.

Consequently, Coetzee's text has the "air of a translation"—and what better tone to generate than that of a translation for this text, which is supposed to be a recovered manuscript, the ancient record of a dead culture? At first the reader may suspect that only Joll's language has been dehumanized, neutralized, and deflated, as in the report he makes to the magistrate after killing the barbarian father: "During the course of the interrogation contradictions become apparent in the prisoner's testimony. Confronted with these contradictions, the prisoner became enraged and attacked the investigating officer. A scuffle ensued during which the prisoner fell heavily against the wall" (6). But the same kind of brutal flatness worms its way into the magistrate's universe as well. As he comes upon the corpse of the barbarian father, he notes: "The grey beard is caked with blood. The lips are crushed and drawn back, the teeth are broken. One eye is rolled back, the other eye-socket is a bloody hole. 'Close it up,' I say. The guard bunches the opening together" (7). Both discourses share short declarative sentences, an emphasis on dead state-of-being verbs, a paucity of adjectives, a journalistic efficiency, a cruel precision, a limited vocabulary pool, a tone of understatement, a tone of legal notices.

If that is so, then they are speaking the *same* language. They are speaking out of the same universe of discourse. In that case, everyone's means of expression, humanity, and individuality has been deactivated. And so once more we are back to Kafka, in whose texts everyone speaks the same way. And we are back to Barthes, who announces the advent of writing degree zero, a negative mood. And we are back to Derrida, where writing is an orphan in search of a father. And we are back to the monologic postmodern fantasies of Borges, Robbe-Grillet, Beckett, Fuentes, Pynchon, and García Márquez, texts that disintegrate before anyone has heard, texts filled with play and freeplay, but also with nostalgia, desire and despair, a recognition that there are fields of blankness, and a desolation that there has to be such blankness.

## 8

# Postlude

> To make the individual *uncomfortable*, that is my task.
> Nietzsche (50)

To sum up briefly, then, clearly something has happened to literature since, roughly, the forties. We can call this state of mind "postmodernism," or we can come up with a less loaded term—perhaps Hassan's Age of Indetermanence, or something else, Absurdism, The Atomic Age, The Television Age, The Age of Kafka, The Age of Uncertainty. Whatever it is called, we find, for better or worse, a new cluster of obsessions: a deconstructive impulse that either takes the form of minimalism, a movement toward silence, exhaustion, degree zero (both existentially and linguistically), and impotence and entropy; or takes the form of maximalism, a movement toward cacophony, replenishment, possibility, energy and freeplay, and joy in plurisignification. Either way this cluster of obsessions includes an acknowledgment of the dehuman, a perversion of contemporary cultural norms, a belief in The End, a radical experimentalism that privileges the way something is being written over what is being written about, unmaking, chance, gaming, a universe of surfaces rather than depth, an intertextuality of misreadings rather than interpretation, acidic irony, and black humor—all employed toward a devaluation, dismemberment, and demystification of the transcendental signifieds of Western culture. Since these obsessions arose in response to a universe the postmoderns perceive as undergoing both physical and metaphysical erasure, and since the postmoderns attempt facing a situation they believe is fantastic, there is little wonder that the mode of discourse chosen as a vehicle for postmodern consciousness is the fantastic.

Fantasy is a metagenre that touches upon romance, fairy tales, pornography, myth, legend, the *nouveau roman*, pulp fiction, science fiction, satire, utopia, dystopia, detective stories, allegory, dream visions, surrealist fiction, gothic novels, expressionist texts, tales of horror, and so on. In its pure form, it is opposed to the dominant culture of dates, times, places, and certainty. It is a mode of discourse that hovers between two other modes: the marvelous (where narrative believes in a coherent ideology of the *over there*, where narrative is shaped by underlying meaning which is independent of the story it expresses, and where it believes in a metaphysics of presence and so is redemptive and compensatory) and the mimetic (where narrative believes in politics, psychology, community, character that is fully rounded, chronology, the specific over the general, and the *here and now*; and where narrative also believes in a compensatory metaphysics of presence—that the word mirrors the world). Because of its hesitation between two universes of discourse, the fantastic confounds and confuses reader response, generates a dialectic that refuses synthesis, explores the unsaid and unseen, and rejects the definitive version of "truth," "reality," and "meaning." Its function as a mode of discourse is to surprise, question, put into doubt, produce anxiety, make active, disgust, repel, rebel, subvert, pervert, make ambiguous, make discontinuous, deform, dislocate, destabilize.

I have discussed the intersection of postmodernism and fantasy in texts by Kafka, Borges, Robbe-Grillet, Beckett, Fuentes, Pynchon, García Márquez, and Coetzee, but there is a host of writers and texts I might have discussed: D. M. Thomas' *White*

*Hotel*, Donald Barthelme's fictions, Ted Mooney's *Easy Travel to Other Planets*, Vladimir Nabokov's *Pale Fire*, Robert Coover's *Public Burning* or *Pricksongs and Descants*, Kurt Vonnegut's *Slaughter-House Five* and other novels, Tim O'Brien's *Going After Cacciato*, Walter Abish's *Alphabetical Africa*, Joseph Heller's *Catch-22*, Italo Calvino's *If on a Winter's Night a Traveler* . . . , Julio Cortázar's short fictions, Günter Grass' *Tin Drum*, and so forth.

In each case, postmodern fantasy becomes the literary equivalent of deconstructionism, for it interrogates all we take for granted about language and experience, giving these no more than a shifting and provisional status. And yet alongside the deconstructive impulse surfaces another, a humanist longing, a humane despair. Along side the freedom of freeplay there arises a nostalgia for the universe of compensation and redemption, the power of the transcendental signified, and the limitations of a metaphysics of presence where the self is coherent and language can say. As a result, postmodern fantasy becomes a mode of radical skepticism and hesitation that believes in the impossibility of total intelligibility; in the endless displacement of "meaning"; in the production of a universe without fault, truth, or origin; in a bottomless relativity of "significance" where, as Barthes notes, we have substituted "for the magisterial space of the past . . . a less upright, less Euclidean space where no one . . . would ever be *in his final place*" (*Image/Music/Text*, 205), a space that disorients the Law, a space of hovering, just like those charming and marvelous UFOs I mentioned at the outset of this study, a space of eternal floating.

# *Bibliography*

### PRIMARY SOURCES

Auden, W. H. *Selected Poems.* New York: Vintage Books, 1979.
Beckett, Samuel. *Collected Poems in English and French.* New York: Grove Press, 1977.
———. *Watt.* New York: Grove Press, 1953.
———. *Waiting for Godot.* New York: Grove Press, 1954.
———. *Stories and Texts for Nothing.* New York: Grove Press, 1967.
———. *Murphy.* New York: Grove Press, 1957.
———. *Molloy, Malone Dies, The Unnamable: Three Novels by Samuel Beckett.* New York: Grove Press, 1958.
———. *Endgame.* New York: Grove Press, 1958.
———. *Happy Days.* New York: Grove Press, 1961.
———. *How It Is.* New York: Grove Press, 1964.
———. *More Pricks Than Kicks.* New York: Grove Press, 1972.
———. *First Love and Other Shorts.* New York: Grove Press, 1974.
———. *Fizzles.* New York: Grove Press, 1976.
———. "All Strange Away." In *Rockaby and Other Short Pieces.* New York: Grove Press, 1981.
———. *Ill Seen, Ill Said.* New York: Grove Press, 1981.
———. *Worstward Ho.* New York: Grove Press, 1983.
Borges, Jorge Luis. *Labyrinths: Selected Stories and Other Writings.* Translated by Donald A. Yates, et al. New York: New Directions, 1964.

———. *Ficciones*. Translated by Emece Editores. New York: Grove Press, 1962.

———. *Doctor Brodie's Report*. Translated by Norman Thomas Di Giovanni. New York: E. P. Dutton, 1978.

Coetzee, J. M. *Dusklands*. New York: Penguin Books, 1982.

———. *In the Heart of the Country*. New York: Penguin Books, 1977.

———. *Waiting for the Barbarians*. New York: Penguin Books, 1980.

Dante Alighieri. *Inferno*. Translated by John D. Sinclair. New York: Oxford University Press, 1980.

Fuentes, Carlos. "In a Flemish Garden." In *Burnt Water*. Translated by Margaret Sayers Peden. New York: Farrar, Straus and Giroux, 1980.

———. *Aura*. Translated by Lysander Kemp. New York: Farrar, Straus and Giroux, 1965.

———. *The Death of Artemio Cruz*. Translated by Sam Hileman. New York: Farrar, Straus and Giroux, 1964.

García Márquez, Gabriel. *Leaf Storm and Other Stories*. Translated by Gregory Rabassa. New York: Avon Books, 1972.

———. *In Evil Hour*. Translated by Gregory Rabassa. New York: Avon Books, 1979.

———. *No One Writes to the Colonel and Other Stories*. Translated by J. S. Bernstein. New York: Harper Colophon Books, 1968.

———. *Innocent Erendira and Other Stories*. Translated by Gregory Rabassa. New York: Harper Colophon Books, 1978.

———. *One Hundred Years of Solitude*. Translated by Gregory Rabassa. New York: Harper & Row, 1970.

———. *The Autumn of the Patriarch*. Translated by Gregory Rabassa. New York: Avon Books, 1975.

———. *Chronicle of a Death Foretold*. Translated by Gregory Rabassa. New York: Alfred A. Knopf, 1983.

Kafka, Franz. *The Penal Colony: Stories and Short Pieces*. Translated by Willa Muir and Edwin Muir. New York: Schocken Books, 1961.

———. *Selected Short Stories of Franz Kafka*. Translated by Willa Muir and Edwin Muir. New York: Modern Library, 1952.

———. *The Trial*. Translated by Willa Muir and Edwin Muir. New York: Modern Library, 1956.

———. *The Castle*. Translated by Willa Muir and Edwin Muir. New York: Modern Library, 1958.

Pynchon, Thomas. V. New York: Bantam Books, 1964.
———. *The Crying of Lot 49*. New York: Bantam Books, 1967.
———. *Gravity's Rainbow*. New York: Viking, 1973.
Robbe-Grillet, Alain. *The Erasers*. Translated by Richard Howard. New York: Grove Press, 1964.
———. *The Voyeur*. Translated by Richard Howard. New York: Grove Press, 1958.
———. *Jealousy*. Translated by Richard Howard. New York: Grove Press, 1979.
———. *In the Labyrinth*. Translated by Richard Howard. New York: Grove Press, 1960.
Stendhal. *The Red and The Black*. Translated by Lloyd C. Parks. New York: The New American Library, 1970.

## SECONDARY SOURCES

Bair, Deirdre. *Samuel Beckett: A Biography*. New York: Harcourt Brace Jovanovich, 1978.
Barrett, William. *Irrational Man: A Study in Existential Philosophy*. New York: Doubleday, 1962.
Barth, John. "The Literature of Exhaustion." *The Atlantic* 220.2 (1967): 29–34.
Barthes, Roland. *Writing Degree Zero*. Translated by Annette Lavers and Colin Smith. New York: Hill and Wang, 1953.
———. *Image/Music/Text*. Translated by Stephen Heath. New York: Hill and Wang, 1977.
Beckett, Samuel. "Three Dialogues." In *Samuel Beckett: A Collection of Critical Studies*, edited by Martin Esslin. Englewood Cliffs: Prentice-Hall, 1965.
Bettelheim, Bruno. *The Uses of Enchantment: The Meaning and Importance of Fairy Tales*. New York: Vintage Books, 1975.
Blanchot, Maurice. "Reading Kafka." Translated by Glenn W. Most. In *Twentieth Century Interpretations of "The Trial,"* edited by James Rolleston. New Jersey: Prentice-Hall, 1976.
Brody, Robert, and Charles Rossman, eds. *Carlos Fuentes: A Critical View*. Austin: University of Texas Press, 1982.
Butler, Christopher. *After the Wake: An Essay on the Contemporary Avant-Garde*. Oxford: Clarendon Press, 1980.
Caramello, Charles. *Silverless Mirrors: Book, Self & Postmodern*

American Fiction. Tallahassee: University of Florida Press, 1983.
Chase, Richard. *The American Novel and Its Tradition.* Baltimore: The Johns Hopkins University Press, 1957.
Chatman, Seymour. *Story and Discourse: Narrative Structure in Fiction and Film.* Ithaca: Cornell University Press, 1978.
Derrida, Jacques. "Structure, Sign and Play in the Discourse of the Human Sciences." No translator given. In *The Structuralist Controversy*, edited by Richard Macksey and Eugenio Donato. Baltimore: The Johns Hopkins University Press, 1972.
Descartes, Rene. *Discourse.* Translated by John Veitch. New York: Dutton, 1937.
Duran, Gloria. *The Archetypes of Carlos Fuentes: From Witch to Androgyne.* Hamden, Conn.: Archon Books, 1980.
Fiedler, Leslie. "The New Mutants." *Partisan Review* 32.4 (1965): 505–25, reprinted in *Collected Essays.* Volume 2. New York: Stein and Day, 1971.
Fletcher, John, and John Spurling. *Beckett: A Study of His Plays.* New York: Hill and Wang, 1972.
Forster, E. M. *Aspects of the Novel.* New York: Harcourt Brace Jovanovich, 1955.
Foster, David William. "Latin American Documentary Narrative." *PMLA* 99.1 (1984): 41–55.
Foucault, Michel. "What is an Author?" In *Textual Strategies: Perspectives in Post-Structuralist Criticism*, edited by Josue V. Harari. Ithaca: Cornell University Press, 1979.
Freud, Sigmund. "Creative Writers and Daydreaming." In *Critical Theory Since Plato*, edited by Hazard Adams. New York: Harcourt Brace Jovanovich, 1971.
Frye, Northrop. *Anatomy of Criticism: Four Essays.* Princeton: Princeton University Press, 1957.
Gallagher, D. P. *Modern Latin American Literature.* London: Oxford University Press, 1973.
Garvin, Harry, ed. *Romanticism, Modernism, Postmodernism.* Lewisburg: Bucknell University Press, 1980.
Gottlieb, Carla. *Beyond Modern Art.* New York: Dutton, 1976.
Guibert, Rita. *Seven Voices: Seven Latin American Writers Talk to Rita Guibert.* Translated by Frances Partridge. New York: Alfred A. Knopf, 1973.

Harss, Luis, and Barbara Dohmann. *Into the Mainstream*. New York: Harper & Row, 1967.
Hassan, Ihab. *The Dismemberment of Orpheus: Toward a Postmodern Literature*. Madison: University of Wisconsin Press, 1982.
―――. *Paracriticisms: Seven Speculations of the Times*. Urbana: University of Illinois Press, 1975.
Howe, Irving. "Mass Society and Postmodern Fiction." *Partisan Review* 26.3 (1959): 420–36. Reprinted in his *Decline of the New*. New York: Harcourt Brace Jovanovich, 1970.
―――. *New York Times Book Review* April 18, 1982: 1.
Hume, Kathryn. *Fantasy and Mimesis: Response to Reality in Western Literature*. New York: Methuen, 1985.
Irwin, William. *The Game of the Impossible: A Rhetoric of Fantasy*. Urbana: University of Illinois Press, 1976.
Jackson, Rosemary. *Fantasy: The Literature of Subversion*. New York: Methuen, 1981.
Jameson, Fredric. "Metacommentary." *PMLA* 86 (1971): 9–17.
Jammer, Max. "Indeterminacy in Physics." *Dictionary of the History of Ideas*. Volume I. New York: Charles Scribner's Sons, 1973.
Janes, Regina. *Gabriel García Márquez: Revolutions in Wonderland*. Columbia: University of Missouri Press, 1981.
Kennard, Jean. *Number and Nightmare: Forms of Fantasy in Contemporary Fiction*. Hamden, Conn.: Archon Books, 1975.
Kenner, Hugh. *Samuel Beckett: A Critical Study*. Berkeley: University of California Press, 1961.
Kermode, Frank. *The Sense of an Ending*. Oxford: Oxford University Press, 1966.
Levin, Harry. "What Was Modernism?" *Massachusetts Review* 1.4 (1960): 609–30. Reprinted in *Refractions*. New York: Oxford University Press, 1966.
Levine, George, and David Leverenz, eds. *Mindful Pleasures: Essays on Thomas Pynchon*. Boston: Little, Brown, 1976.
Lucretius. *On The Nature of the Universe*. Translated by Ronald Latham. New York: Penguin Books, 1979.
Lyotard, Jean-François. *The Postmodern Condition*. Translated by Geoff Bennington and Brian Massumi. Minneapolis: University of Minnesota Press, 1984.
Manlove, C. N. *Modern Fantasy: Five Studies*. Cambridge: Cambridge University Press, 1975.

Marquard, Jean. *Contrast* 12.1 (1983): 45.
Massey, Irving. *The Gaping Pig: Literature and Metamorphosis*. Berkeley: University of California Press, 1976.
McMurray, George R. *Jorge Luis Borges*. New York: Frederick Ungar Publishing Company, 1980.
———. *Gabriel García Márquez*. New York: Frederick Ungar Publishing Company, 1977.
Mendelson, Edward, ed. *Twentieth Century Views: Pynchon*. Englewood Cliffs: Prentice-Hall, 1978.
Monégal, Emir Rodriquez. *Jorge Luis Borges: A Literary Biography*. New York: Dutton, 1978.
Newman, Charles, and Mary Kinzie, eds. *Prose for Borges*. Evanston: Northwestern University Press, 1974.
Newton, Isaac. *Mathematical Principles*. Translated by Andrew Motte. London: Dawson, 1968.
Nietzsche, Friedrich. *The Portable Nietzsche*. Translated and edited by Walter Kaufmann. New York: Penguin Books, 1977.
Ostrowski, Witold. "The Fantastic and The Realistic in Literature." *Zagadnienia rodzajow literackich* 9.1 (1966).
Paz, Octavio. *The Labyrinth of Solitude: Life and Thought in Mexico*. Translated by Lysander Kemp. New York: Grove Press, 1961.
Plato. *The Works of Plato*. Translated by Benjamin Jowett. New York: The Modern Library, 1956.
———. *Timaeus*. Translated by Desmond Lee. New York: Penguin Books, 1979.
Pope, Alexander. "An Essay on Criticism." In *Critical Theory Since Plato*, edited by Hazard Adams. New York: Harcourt Brace Jovanovich, 1971.
Pops, Martin."The Metamorphosis of Shit." *Salmagundi* 56 (1982): 26–61.
Rabkin, Eric. *The Fantastic in Literature*. Princeton: Princeton University Press, 1976.
Robbe-Grillet, Alain. *For A New Novel: Essays on Fiction*. Translated by Richard Howard. New York: Grove Press, 1965.
Rolleston, James, ed. *Twentieth Century Interpretations of "The Trial"*. Englewood Cliffs: Prentice-Hall, 1976.
Roth, Philip. "Writing American Fiction." *Commentary* 31.3 (1961): 223–33.
Sartre, Jean-Paul. " 'Aminadab,' or the Fantastic Considered as Lan-

guage." *Situations*. Translated by Benita Eisler. New York: G. Braziller, 1965.
Schlobin, Roger, ed. *The Aesthetics of Fantasy Literature and Art*. Notre Dame: University of Notre Dame Press, 1982.
Skulsky, Harold. *Metamorphosis: The Mind in Exile*. Cambridge: Harvard University Press, 1981.
Sontag, Susan. *Against Interpretation and Other Essays*. New York: Delta Books, 1981.
Steiner, George. *Language and Silence: Essays on Language, Literature and the Inhuman*. New York: Atheneum, 1982.
———. *The New Yorker* July 12, 1982: 102–3.
Stevick, Philip, ed. *The Theory of the Novel*. New York: The Free Press, 1967.
Swinfen, Ann. *In Defense of Fantasy: A Study of the Genre in English and American Literature Since 1945*. London: Routledge and Kegan Paul, 1984.
Thiher, Allen. *Words in Reflection: Modern Language Theory and Postmodern Fiction*. Chicago: University of Chicago Press, 1984.
———. "Kafka's Legacy." *Modern Fiction Studies* 26.4 (1980–81): 543–62.
Todorov, Tzvetan. *The Fantastic: A Structural Approach to a Literary Genre*. Translated by Richard Howard. New York: Cornell University Press, 1975.
Toynbee, Arnold. *A Study of History*. New York: Oxford University Press, 1947.
Ullmann, Leonard, and Leonard Krasner. *A Psychological Approach to Abnormal Behavior*. Englewood Cliffs: Prentice-Hall, 1975.
Whiteson, Leon. *Canadian Forum* 62 (1982): 8.
Wilde, Alan. *The Horizons of Assent: Modernism, Postmodernism, and the Ironic Imagination*. Baltimore: The Johns Hopkins University Press, 1981.
Wood, J. B. "*Dusklands*: 'The Impregnable Stronghold of the Intellect.' " *Theoria* 54 (1980): 13–23.

# Index

Abish, Walter, 117
*Absalom, Absalom!* (Faulkner), 92
Absence, 9, 12, 19, 23, 36, 43, 65, 80, 86, 94, 98, 100, 101-13
Abstract expressionism, 10
Absurdism, 2, 5, 11, 82, 85, 95, 101, 115
Age of Kafka, 115
Age of Silence, 5
Age of Uncertainty, 5, 115
*All Strange Away* (Beckett), 108
*Alphabetical Africa* (Abish), 117
Antinomianism (Hassan), 8
*Antología de la poesía española e hispano-americana*, 6
Aragon, Louis, 13
Aristotle, 15
*Aspects of the Novel* (Forster), 15
*Aspern Papers, The* (James), 56
Atomic Age, 5, 115
Atomic swerve *(clinamen)*, 73
Auden, W. H., 39, 41
Augustine, Saint, 51

*Aura* (Fuentes), 23, 51-68
Authorial plot, 27-28
Autism, 26-37, 44, 105
*Autumn of the Patriarch, The* (García Márquez), 77, 90, 91, 92-93, 95, 97, 98, 100
"Axolotl" (Cortázar), 54

Balzac, Honoré de, 19
Balzacian mode (Robbe-Grillet), 1, 3, 19, 21, 31, 61, 90-91, 96-97, 98-100, 104
Barrett, William, 75
Barth, John, 2, 16
Barthelme, Donald, 116
Barthes, Roland, 8, 9, 113, 117
Beckett, Samuel, 1, 4, 23, 38, 39-50, 66, 67, 77, 83, 96, 97, 101, 104, 107, 113, 116
"Before the Law" (Kafka), 110
Beethoven, Ludwig von, 2
Behaviorism, 10, 13
Bellemin-Noël, Jean, 21
Bergson, Henri, 30

Bessière, Irène, 20
Bettelheim, Bruno, 15, 28, 96
"Blacaman the Good, Vendor of Miracles" (García Márquez), 92
Blake, William, 13
Blanchot, Maurice, 31
Bodily functions, 39-50
Bohr, Niels, 10, 74
Borges, Jorge Luis, 8, 16, 23, 25-37, 44, 49, 67, 89, 97, 104, 105, 107, 113, 116
*Breath* (Beckett), 49
Breton, André, 13
Brontë, Emily, 18
Burgess, Anthony, 16
Butler, Christopher, 6

Cabrera Infante, G., 89
Cage, John, 49, 99
Caillois, Roger, 20
Calvino, Italo, 117
Caramello, Charles, 4, 6, 7, 9
Carnival, 14
Carpentier, Alejo, 16
*Castle, The* (Kafka), 27, 35
*Catch-22* (Heller), 117
Cervantes Saavedra, Miguel de, 7
Character, 1, 2, 20-21, 61-62, 91-94
Chase, Richard, 21
Chaucer, Geoffrey, 56
Chesterton, Gilbert Keith, 37
Chrétien de Troyes, 18
Christie, Agatha, 82
*Chronicle of a Death Foretold, A* (García Márquez), 97, 99, 100
Coetzee, John M., 23, 45, 100, 101-13, 116
Coleridge, Samuel Taylor, 15

Communal plot, 1, 2, 27-28
Complementarity (Bohr), 10
Computers, 10
Conceptual art, 97
Coover, Robert, 117
Cortázar, Julio, 54, 117
"Creative Writers and Daydreaming" (Freud), 16
*Crying of Lot 49, The* (Pynchon), 19, 69-83

Dali, Salvador, 13, 20, 40
Dante Aligheri, 18, 45, 51-54
Darwin, Charles, 7, 27, 41
*Dead Souls* (Gogol), 82
"Death and the Compass" (Borges), 35
*Death of Artemio Cruz, The* (Fuentes), 55
Deconstructionism, 3, 12, 19-23, 65, 107-12, 115, 117
Deferredness of Meaning (Freudian *Nachträglichkeit*), 31
Defoe, Daniel, 101
Degree zero writing (Barthes), 8, 9, 36, 113, 115
Democritus, 73, 80
Depth psychology, 1, 2, 10, 21-22, 63-64
Derrida, Jacques, 4, 9, 107, 110, 113
Descartes, René, 40, 41, 49-50
Detective story, 31, 65, 75-83, 98, 105, 108
Determinism, 73
Dickens, Charles, 7
*Discourse* (Descartes), 49
*Dismemberment of Orpheus, The* (Hassan), 17

# Index

*Divine Comedy, The* (Dante), 18, 45, 51-54
Dohmann, Barbara, 55, 86-87
Donne, John, 21
Doyle, Arthur Conan, 82
Duchamp, Marcel, 40
*Dusklands* (Coetzee), 101-2

*Easy Travel to Other Planets* (Mooney), 116
*Echo's Bones* (Beckett), 40
Einstein, Albert, 8
Eliot, George, 13
Eliot, T. S., 13, 70, 96
Elitism, 8
Endings, 82-83, 99-100, 108
*Endgame* (Beckett), 108
Entropy, 8, 36, 43, 45, 69, 86, 95, 100, 106, 108, 115
"Enueg I" (Beckett), 40
*Epic of Gilgamesh, The*, 2
Epicurus, 73
*Erasers, The* (Robbe-Grillet), 27, 35
*Essay on Criticism* (Pope), 15
Exhaustion (Barth), 2, 12, 43, 115
*Experimental Novel, The* (Zola), 15
Experimentalism, 13
Expressionism, 5, 13, 97

*Faerie Queene, The* (Spenser), 15
Fantastic, defined, 14-22
Faulkner, William, 7, 23, 56, 90, 92, 101, 117
Federman, Raymond, 11
*Femme Fatale*, 59
Fiedler, Leslie, 6
*Finnegans Wake* (Joyce), 10, 77

Fitts, Dudley, 6
*Fizzles* (Beckett), 42
Flaubert, Gustave, 13, 19
*For A New Novel* (Robbe-Grillet), 2, 30, 31, 33
Forster, E. M., 15
Foucault, Michel, 48
Franco-Prussian War, 58
Freud, Sigmund, 7-8, 10, 11, 16, 21-22, 41
"Frontiers of Criticism: Metaphors of Silence" (Hassan), 6
Frye, Northrop, 21
Fuentes, Carlos, 23, 50, 51-68, 97, 104, 113, 116
"Funes the Memorious" (Borges), 36

Gallagher, D. P., 88-89
Game theory, 33-35, 47, 62, 93, 105
García Márquez, Gabriel, 23, 77, 83, 85-100, 107, 113, 116
Garvin, Harry, 6
"Geography of the House, The" (Auden), 39
Geulincx, Arnold, 50
Gibbon, Edward, 101
Goethe, Johann Wolfgang von, 18
Gogol, Nikolai, 18, 54
*Going After Cacciato* (O'Brien), 117
Golding, William, 16
Gothic novel, 56
Grass, Günter, 117
*Gravity's Rainbow* (Pynchon), 13, 69, 70, 71, 82, 89
"Guayaquil" (Borges), 29

*Hamlet* (Shakespeare), 16
Handke, Peter, 8
"Hans, My Hedgehog" (Bettelheim), 96
*Happy Days* (Beckett), 46
Harlequin romances, 89
Harss, Luis, 55, 86-87
Hassan, Ihab, 5-6, 8, 115
Hawthorne, Nathaniel, 7, 71
Hegel, Georg Wilhelm Friedrich, 100, 104
Heisenberg, Werner, 70, 73-74
Heller, Joseph, 16, 117
Hemingway, Ernest, 13
Hiroshima, 10
Hoffmann, E. T. A., 15, 56
*House of the Seven Gables* (Hawthorne), 7
*How It Is* (Beckett), 48, 104
Howe, Irving, 6, 103-4, 108
Howells, William Dean, 19
Hume, Kathryn, 15, 16
"Hunger Artist, A" (Kafka), 29, 94
Hypnagogic state, 26, 47, 63, 108

*If on a Winter's Night A Traveler . . .* (Calvino), 117
*Ill Seen, Ill Said* (Beckett), 48
"Imperial Message, An" (Kafka), 29
Impressionism, 4, 7
*In the Heart of the Country* (Coetzee), 102, 103
*In the Labyrinth* (Robbe-Grillet), 27, 30, 33, 35-36, 37
Indetermanence (Hassan), 5, 115
Indeterminacy, 5, 12, 19, 23, 43, 68, 69-83, 98-99, 105, 106
Industrialization, 7

*In Evil Hour* (García Márquez), 97, 98, 100
*Interpretation of Dreams, The* (Freud), 7
"Investigations of a Dog" (Kafka), 34
Irwin, William, 17

Jackson, Rosemary, 16, 18
James, Henry, 56
Jameson, Fredric, 1, 4
Janes, Regina, 87
*Jealousy* (Robbe-Grillet), 20, 24, 35, 66
Joyce, James, 13, 42-43, 70, 77, 105
"Judgement, The" (Kafka), 36
Jung, Carl Gustav, 64-65

"Kafka and his Precursors" (Borges), 105
Kafka, Franz, 8, 17, 20, 23, 35-37, 41, 49, 51-54, 63, 76, 78, 94, 95, 96, 97, 99, 101, 104, 105-7, 110, 113, 116
Kandinsky, Wassily, 13
Kavanagh, Thomas, 32
Kelly, Ellsworth, 49
Kennard, Jean, 3, 16
Kenner, Hugh, 43, 46
Kermode, Frank, 31, 99
Kierkegaard, Søren, 74
Kleist, Heinrich von, 18
Kline, Franz, 10
Kooning, Willem de, 10
Krasner, Leonard, 28

*Labyrinth of Solitude, The* (Paz), 94, 95-96

# Index

*Labyrinths* (Borges), 25
Language, 8, 9, 10, 12, 21, 36-37, 42-50, 86, 94, 98-99, 104-5, 106-7, 109-13, 117
Laplace, Pierre Simon, 74
"Last Voyage of the Ghost Ship, The" (Garcia Marquez), 94-95
*Leafstorm* (García Márquez), 87, 88, 90, 91, 92, 94, 97, 100
*Leaves of Grass* (Whitman), 7
Levin, Harry, 6
"Library of Babel, The" (Borges), 32, 34, 35, 37
"Literature of Exhaustion, The" (Barth), 2
*Lost Ones, The* (Beckett), 44
Lucretius, 73
Lyotard, Jean-François (Metanarrative), 6, 11

Magical realism, 16
Mangel, Anne, 70
Manlove, C. N., 16, 17
Manzoni, Piero, 41
Márquez. See "García Márquez."
Marvelous, defined, 18-19
Marquard, Jean, 103-4
*Masked Days, The* (Fuentes), 56
Marx, Karl, 7, 11, 100
"Mass Society and Postmodern Fiction" (Howe), 6
Massey, Irving, 51-54
Maximalism, 8-9, 10, 115
Maxwell's Demon, 69
McMurray, George, 87
Melville, Herman, 7, 8
Menippean Satire, 14
Metadiscourse, 13

*Metamorphoses* (Ovid), 73, 80, 105
Metamorphosis, 23, 45, 51-68
*Metamorphosis, The* (Kafka), 17, 28-29, 36, 51-54, 95
Metanarrative (Lyotard), 13
Metaphysics of absence (Derrida), 107-12
Metaphysics of presence (Derrida), 107-12, 117
Metatext, 13
Mimesis, defined, 18-19
Minimalism, 8-9, 10, 43, 97, 115
Miró, Joan, 40
Misrule, 14
*Moby-Dick* (Melville), 7
Modernism, defined, 7-8
Mooney, Ted, 116
*More Pricks than Kicks* (Beckett), 45
Moréas, Jean, 7
Munch, Edvard, 13
Murdoch, Iris, 16
*Murphy* (Beckett), 41, 44, 50

"Nabo" (García Márquez), 90, 91
Nabokov, Vladimir, 59, 117
Narrative frustration, 23, 82-83, 85-100
*National Enquirer, The*, 1
"New Mutants, The" (Fiedler), 6
New Realism, 97
Newman, Barnett, 49
New Physics, 70, 72-75
Newtonian mechanics, 7, 8
*New York Times Book Review*, 103
Nietzsche, Friedrich, 96-97, 115
Night journey (Jung), 64-65

"Night of the Curlews, The" (García Márquez), 87
*Night of the Living Dead* (Romero), 21
Nohrnberg, James, 82-83
*Nose, The* (Gogol), 54
Novella, 56

Objective correlative, 30
O'Brien, Tim, 117
"Old Manuscript, An" (Kafka), 36, 105-106
*On the Nature of the Universe* (Lucretius), 73
"One Day After Saturday" (García Márquez), 87
*One Hundred Years of Solitude* (García Márquez), 85, 90-91, 92, 93, 95-96, 97, 98, 100
Onís, Federico de, 6
Op art, 67-68, 97
Ostrowski, Witold, 44
"Other Side of Death, The" (García Márquez), 92
Ovid, 53, 73, 80

*Pale Fire* (Nabokov), 117
Pavlov, Ivan Petrovich, 10
Paz, Octavio, 94, 95-96
Peirce, Charles Sanders, 73
Periodization, limitations of, 4
Peripeteia, 99
Petronius, 82
Planck, Max, 8
Plato, 15, 72, 74, 80-81
Pla(y)gerism (Federman), 11
Poe, Edgar Allan, 18, 20, 56
Pollock, Jackson, 10, 40
Pop art, 97

Pope, Alexander, 15
Postmodernism, defined, 4-14
*Pricksongs and Descants* (Coover), 117
Primitivism, 8
*Principia* (Newton), 73
Proust, Marcel, 96, 105
Psychology. *See* Behaviorism, Depth Psychology, Character, Balzacian mode
*Public Burning, The* (Coover), 116
Pushkin, Alexander, 56
Pynchon, Thomas, 8-9, 13, 19, 23, 45, 63, 68, 69-83, 88, 96, 97, 100, 104, 113, 116

Quark physics, 10-11
*Queen of Spades* (Pushkin), 56

Rabelais, François, 83
Rabkin, Eric, 16, 17
Reader's role in postmodern fantasy, 30-34, 63, 65, 67-68, 76-83, 85-100
"Reading Kafka" (Blanchot), 31
Realism, 1, 2, 4, 13, 41. *See also* Mimesis.
Relativity theory, 8, 70
Renard, Jules, 42
*Republic, The* (Plato), 15
Rilke, Rainer Maria, 105
Robbe-Grillet, Alain, 1, 2, 19, 20, 23, 25-37, 44, 47, 66, 76, 99, 97, 101, 104, 113, 115
Romanticism, 5, 13
Romero, George, 21
"Rose for Emily, A" (Faulkner), 156

# Index

Roth, Philip, 14
Rothko, Mark, 49

Sade, Marquis de, 4
"Sanies I" (Beckett), 40
"Sanies II" (Beckett), 40
Sartre, Jean-Paul, 19, 47
Satire, 14, 82-83
*Satyricon* (Petronius), 82
Schlobin, Roger, 16
Scholes, Robert, 15
Schrödinger, Erwin, 73
Scott, Walter, 15
Selfhood, 2, 43, 45-48, 54, 58-62, 64-65, 67, 91-92, 117
Shelley, Mary Godwin, 18, 21
Sidney, Philip, 15
Singer, Isaac Bashevis, 71-72
Skulsky, Harold, 51-54
*Slaughter-House Five* (Vonnegut), 117
Socrates, 72
Solitude, 94-96
Sontag, Susan, 32
Sophocles, 79-80, 175
Sorrentino, Gilbert, 8
Soto, Jesús-Rafäel, 68
"South, The" (Borges), 27, 30
Space age, 5
Spanish Civil War, 10
Spenser, Edmund, 15
Sputnik, 10
Stalinist Purges, 10
*Star Wars* (Spielberg and Lucas), 18
Steiner, George, 11, 104
Stendhal, 19
Sterne, Laurence, 7, 10, 83
Stevens, Wallace, 13

Stevenson, Robert Louis, 54, 56
*Stories and Texts for Nothing* (Beckett), 48
*Strange Case of Dr. Jekyll and Mr. Hyde, The* (Stevenson), 54, 56
*Study of History, A* (Toynbee), 6
Surrealism, 13, 43, 59
Swift, Jonathan, 41, 100
Swinfen, Ann, 14, 16, 17
Symbolist movement, 7


Teaching postmodern fantasy, 82, 90
Technologism (Hassan), 8
*Temps Humain* (Bergson), 30
Television, 10
Television Age, 5, 115
Tennyson, Alfred Lord, 7
Texticide (Thiher), 100
Thackery, William Makepeace, 7
Thiher, Allen, 6, 7, 100, 105
Thomas, D. M., 116
*Timaeus* (Plato), 72
Time, 20, 30, 66, 96-97, 108
*Tin Drum, The* (Grass), 117
"Tlactocazine, The One from the Flemish Garden" (Fuentes), 56
"Tlön, Uqbar, Orbis Tertius" (Borges), 27, 29, 30, 32, 107
Todorov, Tzvetan, 15, 17-18
Tolkien, J. R. R., 15
Toynbee, Arnold, 6
Transcendental signified, 13, 100, 115-16, 117
*Trial, The* (Kafka), 26, 34, 35, 78
Trilogy (Beckett), 1, 41, 45-48, 77, 83, 89
*Tristram Shandy* (Sterne), 7, 10

Ullmann, Leonard, 28
Ultraism, 26
Uncanny, 18-19
Uncertainty. *See* Indeterminacy.
Uncertainty principle, 70, 73-75
Urbanization, 7-8

V (Pynchon), 69, 71, 78
Van Gogh, Vincent, 13
Vargas Llosa, Mario, 89
"Very Old Man With Enormous Wings, The" (García Márquez), 94
Victorianism, 7
Vonnegut, Kurt, 16, 117
*Voyeur, The* (Robbe-Grillet), 27, 30

Waiting, 45, 80, 107
*Waiting for Godot* (Beckett), 46, 49, 107
*Waiting for the Barbarians* (Coetzee), 101-13

Watson, John Broadus, 24
*Watt* (Beckett), 43-45, 66
"What was Modernism?" (Levin), 6
*White Hotel, The* (Thomas), 116
White noise, 69
Whiteson, Leon, 103-04, 108, 112
Whitman, Walt, 7
*Whoroscope* (Beckett), 40
"Wife of Bath, The" (Chaucer), 56
Wilde, Alan, 6, 11
Wilkins, John, 37
Winston, Mathew, 71
Wittgenstein, Ludwig, 69
World War II, 6, 10
*Worstward Ho* (Beckett), 46

Yeats, W. B., 70, 96
*Yvain* (Chrétien), 18

Zola, Émile, 13, 15

## About the Author

LANCE OLSEN is Assistant Professor of English at the University of Kentucky. His numerous articles, short stories, and reviews have appeared in *Modern Language Studies, Sub-Stance, South Atlantic Review, The Iowa Review, The Chicago Review,* and a wide variety of other journals.

DISCARDED

BETHANY COLLEGE LIBRARY